Endorsements

"When an extraordinarily gifted and skilled writer offers essays on the contemplative dimensions of life, we would all do well to pay attention. This collection evokes St. Francis (of course), Annie Dillard, Richard Rohr, and Thomas Merton, but it also rings with Therese DesCamp's unique voice and wisdom. Highly recommended!"

Brian D. McLaren, author of *Life After Doom* and *Faith After Doubt*.

"I didn't know I had been thirsting until I discovered I was drinking at your waterfall. Applause!"

Joy Kogawa, international award-winning poet and author of *Obasan*.

"*Hands Like Roots* is an extraordinary work of hope in a moment that often feels completely bereft of hope. Honest, perceptive and beautifully written, this book serves as a reminder of how important it can be to pay close attention to the minute particulars of our lives. Such attention, as practiced by Therese DesCamp in this wonderful book, becomes a vital and necessary spiritual practice, capable of returning us to our bodies, the living world and one another."

Douglas E. Christie, Ph.D., author of *The Blue Sapphire of the Mind: Notes for a Contemplative Ecology*.

"This sweet, bruising, and brutally honest tome offers a framework for living in (and growing through) turbulent, troubling times. With deep insight from rooted contemplation, she sings a song of hope for the new world that is beckoning us."

Carla A. Grosch-Miller (Revd. Dr.), author of *Psalms redux: Poems and Prayers*, and *Lifelines: Wrestling the Word, Gathering up Grace*.

"This is a splendid book -- foundational and funny, poetic and practical -- essential spiritual nourishment for weary hearts. 'Loving or not loving is a choice,' as DesCamp writes, so if you are among those who have chosen to keep loving this beautiful, aching world, you need this book."

Dr. Mardi Tindal, former Moderator of The United Church of Canada, and Circle of Trust facilitator for the Center for Courage and Renewal.

"...this book reminds us that being contemplative is not adding 30 minutes of meditation to an already busy schedule. DesCamp offers a view of an entangled contemplative life where we remember that it's not our job to figure out exactly how humanity will get out of this mess. Rather, we are called to let go of our own need to understand and to control and, instead, to incarnate faithfulness in whatever situation we find ourselves in."

Bishop Anna Greenwood-Lee, Anglican Bishop of the Diocese of British Columbia.

"*Hands Like Roots: Notes on an Entangled Contemplative Life* is a beautifully woven meditation on the interconnectedness of spiritual practice, daily living, and the natural world. With depth and lyricism, Therese invites readers into a contemplative way of being that is both grounded and expansive, rooting us in presence while opening us to mystery. This book is a profound companion for those seeking to live with greater awareness, wisdom, and grace."

Heather Ruce, Family Systems and Trauma Therapist, Wisdom Teacher, Wisdom Spiritual Director, Sacred Movements Guide.

"It would be gift enough for Therese to come alongside with generous attentiveness to share in our mutual intention to 'let life live through us,' but she has also brought her skill as witness, storyteller, and lyricist to cast a spell and hold my distractible attention to things that matter most in our world right now. Praise be!"

Tim Scorer, Canadian spiritual guide and author of *Experiencing the Heart of Christianity.*

Hands Like Roots

Hands Like Roots

Notes on an Entangled Contemplative Life

Therese DesCamp

SANTOS BOOKS
EVERY STORY SACRED

I dedicate this book to all those who have held their post wholeheartedly, in anonymity, steadfastly. My mother, Jean Marienne Lemieux DesCamp, tops this list. I give thanks to the Contemplative in the Kootenays group for our years of work together; to all my teachers, especially Cynthia Bourgeault; and to my dear partner, best friend, and brilliant photographer George Meier—he sees me clearly.

Contents

Foreword by Alanna Mitchell

The first time I encountered the fierce and tender intellect that is Therese DesCamp, we were at a conference in Vancouver. It was 2012. I was on stage talking about a narrative non-fiction book I had recently written called *Sea Sick*, trying to figure out how to wind down after four sessions spread over as many days. Winding down something like that is the hard part. The book is about how the carbon load in the atmosphere is affecting the ocean – it's an awful story – and I felt my task was to leave the audience with some glimmer of hope.

Finally, I resorted to posing a question. "Is transformation possible?" I asked. Then I paused. "It's a trick question. Transformation is only possible if you believe it's possible."

Therese loved it. She wrote to me later. "As a cognitive linguist, I wanted to stand up and shout YES!!! The frame that you use to view the world absolutely determines what you are capable of seeing; it shapes your reality." And then, of course, being Therese, she appended a research video demonstrating the point.

And so began more than a dozen years of episodic conversations that seemed to revolve around the same theme: the story we tell matters. Telling it matters. It's important to convince yourself to keep telling it, even if that means excavating your innermost suffering.

Hands Like Roots: Notes on an Entangled Contemplative Life is a testament to the power of the story, of the telling, of the excavation. It is about the value of plumbing one's own depths and finding the meaning within. Because as clear as Therese is that her spiritual and emotional work is important, she also knows that it is mainly important because it opens her up for what's going on in the world at large. It is a frame, but not a container.

The frame for this book is an interpretation by Daniel Ladinsky of a short prayer by St. Francis of Assisi. Therese turned St. Francis's four deceptively simple lines into a savagely intelligent contemplation on how to respond to the grief of our "lovely, battered world." That piece originally appeared in 2024 in a climate-themed issue of the Canadian magazine *Broadview* for which I was the commissioning editor. And then she took that frame and magicked it open, big enough to encompass the years' worth of essays that you are now holding in your hands.

But it would be wrong to leave you with the impression that Therese is only about ideas. Her hands, her feet, her heart are firmly planted in the physicality of our planet. And she writes about this, beautifully, always on the lookout for what it all means. Consider the parable of the plum tree in her front yard. A scrawny, ancient thing with gaunt branches, it gave birth to boxes and boxes of deep purple fruit. Rather than merely rejoice in the bounty, Therese has to ask why, only to discover that this unlikely abundance is probably the last-ditch effort of a creature desperate to produce offspring, rather than a sign of its health. Talk about a frame.

I remember when Therese visited me in Toronto just as I was birthing a play based on my book *Sea Sick*. Writing it, which I did with the help of two theatre directors, was hard enough. Worse was the fact that I had to perform it. Therese was to be present at the very first public reading. The play wasn't finished. I hadn't memorized it. Minutes before I went on stage, I was in a toilet stall, literally sick with fear. Therese, valiant, pastoral, simply held me and listened, open to whatever would come. It was, and is, an extraordinarily difficult thing to do, but I have concluded that she knows no other way to show up in the world. Listen. Be. Find your frame.

It amuses me, therefore, that toward the end of this book, she talks about herself as a doula, a handmaid to birth, the one willing to love and carry on when things seem hopeless, the one who is certain that new life is nigh. Yes on all counts. But I am also fixated on another symbol that infuses this book: the fungus. Therese was reading *Entangled Life: How Fungi Make Our Worlds, Change Our Minds & Shape Our Futures*, Merlin Sheldrake's masterpiece about the science of fungi, when she found the prayer that forms the name of this book.

Fungi are just hands-down fascinating. For example, when they combine symbiotically with other creatures to form lichen, it is the fungi that hold the power to shift into the lichen form. Fungi hold the memory for metamorphosis.

Therese cites the quizzical role of fungi in transporting things between trees, mediated by mycorrhizal threads in the soil. Scientists have only recently begun to understand these connections. The plants feed the fungi. The fungi give the plants water, minerals and other nutrients. They are symbionts, dependent on each other and serving one another.

But maybe most fascinating of all, the mycorrhizal network moves information, perhaps even what Canadian botanist Suzanne Simard refers to as a forest's "emergent values." These species share resources. They learn. They have memory. They recognize kin and sacrifice their own well-being for that of others. In humans, this could be called a moral structure. Or a narrative. Or a frame.

Not just doula, then, Therese, but metamorphoser, symbiont, storyteller, teacher to us all.

Alanna Mitchell
Toronto, 2025

Preface

Twenty years ago, in a fit of wild openness, my husband and I decided to move—not just to another city or state, but to another country. It didn't happen all at once, but about three years after the initial spasm, I found myself transplanted (alone; it took him two and a half years to finish up his work) from the Central California coast where I had a job and a title and important things to do, to the outskirts of a tiny village in the inland mountains of British Columbia, where I knew no one. In the interim, we had bought land, designed and built a retreat center, and convinced ourselves that we could make a living conducting and hosting retreats.

The final move occurred in mid-January, while the entire West Coast of North America was blanketed in ice and snow. After three days of slip-slide driving, it was time to cross Snoqualmie Pass, east of Seattle. I had pulled off the road and was lying in the snow, attempting to put chains on the car. Across the median strip, jack-knifed trucks blocked the entire westbound lane. My hands were turning blue, and snow was melting down my neck as I repeated desperately, "I chose this. I still choose this." I repeated that phrase often over the next several years.

We were wrong about the viability of the retreat center. A dream and a business plan are not at all the same things. It just took us ten years to learn that. The purpose of the move appears to have been, from this vantage point, to strip away things that needed to be lost so that something new could come in.

Except I'm not exactly sure what the new is. But that is the nature of *new*, after all. The Spirit blows where She will. It seems enough now to just try to listen and to follow. What I follow is something that some of us call the Christ but you could as easily call the Red Thread: love that's not tied to a specific person or object, but which binds me to life and blows my heart open so wide that everything belongs. Wholeheartedness, Incarnational Love, the Christ, the Way of Compassion—whatever you call it, that's what I try to sense and to follow.

The essays in this book are markers from points along my journey, arranged in response to the short prayer by St. Francis of Assisi that appears at the start of this book. If I arranged them in chronological order, you might observe that the nature of my language about God has changed. So has the name of our current dog. I didn't arrange them in chronological order because, like most people I know, I have cycled through the same realizations over and over, each time wearing the groove of knowing a little more deeply into my heart and consciousness. The specific learnings around which I've grouped my writing—understanding how connected I am in this world, learning to see beauty even where I don't, learning to let go and to pray, and then learning to trust in Divine Wisdom—constitute the heart of my spiritual life. Of course, these practices don't occur in isolation—they are entangled. I have learned to love what I don't love, in part, by letting go of my need for control. But I've tried to share how a given practice works in my life in the hope that you'll hear echoes of your own life.

My hope for you, the reader of this book, is that something you read here will move you toward wholeheartedness: ignite your inner fire, help you grasp the red thread more firmly, awaken the Christ heart of your own life. I imagine you wouldn't be reading this if you didn't already have a longing for this. That longing doesn't mean that something is lacking in you. That longing is the indication that the Holy is alive in you. Notice that.

Now, about religion. You may notice that I am Christian—broadly so. The "broadly so" part has gotten broader over the years, while the Christian part has gotten deeper. More accurately, I

am a contemplative Christian who learns from and values other traditions. This has been a gradual learning for me, reflected in part in
some of these essays. For me personally, Jesus is the express elevator,
but that is surely not true for many whom I love and respect.

A word about language: I've struggled over the years to find a
way to speak of the Unknowable. It's really impossible, in a world
as diverse as this, to find a common language or understanding
about the Ultimate. Some of us find our meaning in earth and sky;
some in synagogue, mosque, sangha, or church; some in the endless
cycle of life or music or the well-turned word. When I use the word
God, it is as a broad metaphor for that which you find central to life
itself. It's simply a whole lot shorter than saying "The-Love-that-
Pulses-at-the Center-of-the-Universe" or "That-Which-Knits-All-
Things-in-Love" or "The-Singularity-Before-the-Big-Bang."
(However, I never mean "the old guy in the bathrobe.") So, I invite
you to translate that loaded word *God* into whatever works best for
you, whatever it is or whoever it is that holds and grounds your own
heart and soul.

One more word about language: I use some. I hope it doesn't
get in the way. As a grown-up Catholic schoolgirl, a little swearing
feels like relish on the dish.

Our hands imbibe like roots
So I place them on what is beautiful in this world.
And I fold them in prayer, and they
draw from the heavens
light.

—St. Francis of Assisi,
Interpreted by Daniel Ladinsky

PART I: OUR HANDS
IMBIBE LIKE ROOTS

{ 1 }

Hands Like Roots

As the forest fires burned a few kilometers away, as around the world dams broke, wars escalated, and political rhetoric sharpened, I struggled to find a quiet heart. My practice—reading, scripture, meditation, prayer—was hard to maintain. Yet I knew that if I continued to show up, practice would serve as a trail through the dark woods of despair, leading me to the space where I could remember that I am rooted in Christ. I needed that trail every day, because my serenity got blown to pieces every day.

+++ +++ +++

For months, I had been working my way through Merlin Sheldrake's masterpiece, *Entangled Life*, about the science of fungi. I read a few paragraphs each morning and pondered them in light of my faith. Early one smoky August day, I finally reached the epilogue, which began with a portion of a short prayer from St. Francis of Assisi. "Our hands imbibe like roots," it read, "So I place them on what is beautiful in this world." My heart quickened. I looked up the footnote, tore through my bookcases, found Daniel Ladinsky's *Love Poems from God*, and read the last two lines in his beautiful interpretation of this prayer: "And I fold them in prayer, and they draw from the heavens light."[1]

I sat back, feeling like I had been given the complete contemplative manifesto for this climate of catastrophe: a template for working with grief, an outline of how to act. So, I start this essay with gratitude. Thank you, Francis of Assisi. Thank you, Daniel Ladinsky. Thank you, Merlin Sheldrake.

And then I turn to the prayer, to the practice.

Our hands imbibe like roots...

First, I notice the words. Francis starts with the collective: "Our hands." Like "Our Father," the first-person plural in this short prayer reminds us of our communal experience. Francis is discussing the universal human reality that we have been created to be in relationship with each other and with the world around us—and more than relationship, really: We are created to drink each other in. We are intended to knit ourselves together with each other.

It's a lovely thing, this embrace of our incarnational selves. We aren't the masters, above and better than all else. Nor are we the parasites who deserve to die. We are simply and beautifully part of the whole.

I take that in: I am a beloved, entangled being, part of a web of beloved, entangled beings.

"Our hands imbibe like roots." This intoxicating line evokes the way that tree roots symbiotically entwine with mycorrhizal fungi to transport nutrients and information between trees. At times, the roots and the fungi are so tightly woven together as to be indistinguishable, with fungi actually residing within the body of the root. The health of the trees and the health of the fungi depend on this relationship with each other.

Then I realize that it's not just roots that imbibe. When I breathe out, the spruce tree outside my window inhales that breath. When that spruce exhales oxygen, I breathe it in. This remarkable cycle of breath sustains both of us. The health of the tree and my health depend on this relationship. This remarkable cycle of breath sustains *all* living creatures.

From the ways that my breath is woven into the world, I move to pondering the rest of my body. I am host to myriad life forms, and these life forms shape my health and life. I eat plants and animals, tiny animals will decompose my body when I die, and plants use that decomposed matter as food. We are woven together in life and in death.

We are also woven into the world mentally. As open-loop neural systems, every mind learns from the minds around it. My mind is restructured by reading your book or hearing your speech. But I also learn from you when you hum the baby a lullaby, when you post an angry comment, or when I walk by a garden that you have tended.

There is, of course, a downside to all this connectedness. It is impossible to distance ourselves from the physical and mental world in which we are entwined. When the trees burn on the mountainside above me, I feel the flames licking at my bark. When earthquakes strike, I am searching the rubble for my toddler. When drought reduces the creek to a trickle, I lie gasping in the mud. When bombs fall, I am praying that my teenagers come safely home.

Being intertwined—imbibing like roots—means that I will take in the innocent suffering of the world. Being intertwined means that there are times when the sorrow overtakes me. It means that I cannot—I will not—stand untouched as Creation groans and writhes like a woman in labor.

As the writer and activist Rebecca Solnit writes, it is possible to be "hopeful and heartbroken at the same time," which brings me to beauty.[2]

So I place them on what is beautiful in this world...
Again, I look closely at the words. Now, it's no longer a story about the collective human experience. Francis says, "I place them." He suggests that the individual can take specific action.

The contemplative teacher Cynthia Bourgeault tells a story about a friend of hers—a jazz musician and Buddhist—who made his living tutoring kids four hours a day, six days a week. Bourgeault once asked him if he got bored. He said he did sometimes, but only when "I'm not paying enough attention."[3]

Attention is the ingredient that lights up the world.

To "place" something requires careful and intentional movement: attention. Placing my hands on the world implies that I enter into relationship with it. It's more than just physical contact. It's conscious awareness. It's reverence.

I decide to take my attention out for a walk. I place my hands on cedar trees and stay until I can feel the warmth and softness of their bark. I rub the scars made by bear claws on a mountain ash trunk. I feel the coolness and grit of the garden soil, smell the pitch on a pine. I rest my eyes on the lavender and gold of Michaelmas daisies. I squeeze a rosehip, rub its waxiness on my palm, taste its tang. I tunnel my fingers into the soft fur of the dog.

I place my hands on beauty. When I pay attention to beauty, it eases the band of anxiety and grief around my chest.

But then I start thinking. What about things that I don't instinctively find beautiful? Francis of Assisi famously experienced conversion when he kissed a leper, writing, "What had previously nauseated me became the source of spiritual and physical consolation for me."[4] When Francis says, "I place them on what is beautiful in this world," I strongly doubt that he means for us to touch only pretty things. I suspect he's suggesting that we learn to see beauty in all things.

I have learned that when I lay my hands on things that aren't inherently attractive, my attention can make them so. As I give my conscious, loving attention to the dirty dishes, to the irritating colleague, to the lengthy board meeting, these become imbued with beauty. "I clean this teapot," said the late Buddhist teacher Thich Nhat Hanh, "with the kind of attention I would have were I giving the baby Buddha or Jesus a bath."[5] When I have taken the time to admire the iridescence and complexity of a stinkbug, how could I possibly harm it? My attention transforms not only my seeing, but also my relationships in the world.

At this point, I stop. I have been drinking in beauty and connection, through my mind, my hands, my eyes and ears, through taste and smell. Now it is time to pay attention to the palpable grateful-ness within. I slow down and let gratitude for this world, as it is this very minute, rise in me. I feel the internal spaciousness that accompanies gratitude. I rest in this.

Gratitude is not only a lovely practice. It is also a necessary accompaniment to what comes next.

Because another question rises when we speak about beauty: What of human evil, senseless destruction? What of the atrocities in Palestine and Israel, the murdered Amazonian land protectors, toxic residue spilling into clean waters? To simply step back and name these as beautiful—arguing that "God must have a reason" or "In a million years it won't matter"—can be the worst kind of spiritual bypassing. The willful refusal to acknowledge pain and suffering is a betrayal of the spiritual path. It is sin.

I don't believe that we are invited to see these horrors as beautiful. I believe, rather, that we are to see *through* every suffering being to the Christ within: to beauty. We are to see that everyone who is tending to suffering beings has a core of Christ, of beauty. We are even to recognize that in the depths of every seemingly soulless perpetrator of destruction resides the suffering Christ, longing to come awake.

Now comes the painful grieving part. Because, of course, to see through the devastated world to the Christ within requires that we look closely at that devastated world first. It requires that we pay attention to what is happening. The problem here is that when I truly pay attention to what's happening in the world, I feel like I might just drown in sorrow. My heart is open, awake, and raw. What do I do with these feelings?

Well, I don't run from them. After all, Jesus wept. So I turn back to the words.

And I fold them in prayer...

Francis tells us that we should take our beautifully sensitive hands and bring them together in prayer. He invites us into a conscious gesture of devotion and humility. Folding my hands in prayer quiets my body and mind. It also reminds me that I am not in charge. I am asking for help from the One who loves me.

I notice, as I follow Francis's directions and fold my hands, that I have ceased taking things in. I have allowed my mind to come to a standstill. I have let go. And when I let go, when I surrender, when the commentary of my busy brain stops, then I really *feel* all this pain. Then my heart *really* breaks.

In my experience, the prayer that accompanies the breaking of my heart does not hew to recognized theological formulas. It is inept, inadequate, and bumbling. It is almost always inarticulate. I recognize that I can't do a damned thing about most of what breaks my heart, and what I *can* do feels so inadequate that I am tempted to quit before I start. I cry for justice, for mercy, for forgiveness, sometimes without a clue about what these might be in the given situations or how they might come to pass. Heartbroken prayer pushes me up against my poverty and powerlessness. I weep. I weep, and, at some point, I shut up.

"I cover my mouth with my hand," said Job.[6] Like Job, I reach the place where I have nothing to say, no useful thoughts to think, no more tears to cry, no inkling what to do next. I surrender.

That's what makes this prayer so powerful.

Because, like Job, when I stop talking, when I let go, then there's room for God.

+++ +++ +++

The first thing that arises as I come to rest in Holy Silence is a re-minder that nothing can separate me from the love of God in Christ Jesus. Neither floods nor fires nor political upheaval nor cata-strophic climate change nor even death can take away the knowl-edge and the experience that we all—every being, every molecule—partake in the life of God. This is the message: At the deepest, truest level, all is beloved. *I* am beloved.

The second thing that comes is the sense that I am being loosened from my mental bondage. I begin to experience freedom from my limited ideas and opinions, my need to have things fixed in a way that I understand. I start to give up attempting to control situations that are beyond my control. I cease trying to figure out if or how we will ever get out of this mess, and—this is the important part!—I be-gin to wonder what faithful response is required of me.

The alternative to all my distraction, confusion, and despair is resting in the stillness of Love. In that quiet center, fear loses its grip on me. It's true that I may still be deeply sad. I am also free to act. This is an interesting way to feel in the midst of heartbreak.

When I let go more deeply into Holy Silence, I recognize that while the world is not mine to fix—after all, I'm not God—some parts of the world *are* mine. There are specific places where I am in-vited to join my human energy to the Holy Intention. "By inner per-suasions, [God] draws us to a few very definite tasks, *our* tasks, God's burdened heart particularizing [God's] burdens in us," wrote the Quaker mystic Thomas R. Kelly.[7] It is this shifting of focus—away from my own sorrow, pain, and fear and toward an inner surrender to infinite, inexplicable Love—that allows me to become bold and free in my actions.

It's not simply about moving my attention away from fear and onto God. It's also about moving away from the endless list of what needs to be done and toward what the Buddhist environmentalist

Joanna Macy describes as "the vision that calls us most strongly."[8] There is no need to do everything. This is a time to trust that others are stepping forward too. Our work will be interwoven and cumulative. We simply and humbly take on the tasks that have been laid upon our own hearts.

When we navigate by heart—not emotion, but the wisdom deep inside—then success ceases to be the measure by which we evaluate our work. If we discern, and faithfully do, what is ours to do, then the important question isn't, "Can we save this old-growth forest?" or "Can we stop this war?" or "Does my work actually make a difference?" The only question that matters is, "Am I being faithful?"

With faithfulness as my standard, divine possibility blossoms in every seemingly dead corner of the world. When faithfulness is our standard, then our work—however seemingly hopeless—will change the world because, as Francis says, there is something more at work.

And they draw from the heavens light.

I return to the prayer, turning my attention once more to the words. It's worth noticing that Francis has again shifted the subject. He began by referencing our collective self, the reality of being a human: "Our hands." He then turned to individual actions that we use to pay attention and to surrender: "I place [my hands and]...fold them in prayer." Now, he directs us to notice that our hands, folded in prayer, cause something to happen: "They draw from the heavens light."

Hands folded in prayer are sacramental. They act as an outward physical expression of an inner surrendered self. It is the humility and devotion expressed by folded hands that draws light from the heavens—not our minds, not our hard work, not our personalities, not our gifts, but the act of turning ourselves and all our concerns over to the Holy. Our surrendered self makes room for something more than us. This is where the Spirit shows up.

Here's the thing about the Spirit: She blows where She will. Once we invite the Spirit in, we don't know what is going to come next. We are accountable for responding faithfully to what has been laid on our hearts. She's in charge of adding the oomph to our actions, putting backbone into our fearful selves, finding us allies—for whatever is needed, for whatever comes next.

+++ +++ +++

In case you're wondering, this is where joy shows up. Joy is what happens when we quit pretending that we deserve to escape this communal suffering. Joy is what happens when, in order to help others, we commit to finding our footing in the flood. Joy is the unintended but inevitable result of heartfelt action: not the reason why we do this work, nor the reward for it, but the side effect of our committed life. Joy rises from the crucible of conscious action like bubbles off champagne, spray from a waterfall, the tang of sourdough bread. As the American poet and author Ross Gay writes, joy is not "a refuge or relief from heartbreak" but rather "what effloresces from us as we help each other carry our heartbreaks."[9]

Our hands imbibe like roots, says Francis. We take in the glory of incarnate life. We touch it and love it and are grateful. We weep over the broken world, and we hold it in the light of God's love. Then we act in faith—not faith that the world isn't really broken, but faith that we are capable of responding because the Holy One really is our root and our ground, holding all things in love, holding all things in relationship.

+++ +++ +++

[1]Daniel Ladinsky, "Like Roots," *Love Poems from God: Twelve Sacred Voices from the East and West* (Penguin Compass, 2002), 40.

[2]Rebecca Solnit, "We Can't Afford to Be Climate Doomers," *The Guardian*, July 26, 2023, https://www.theguardian.com/commentis-free/2023/jul/26/we-cant-afford-to-be-climate-doomers?mkt_tok=Nzc0LVNITy0yMjgAAAGNy8SZL-3_mQ-SOd6ixbsHGyhQJQ4_WmNrumjXDLW9oMh-Lacc3ioSr2w2gpbC0t4C8fvMa3LpjXpVsnNnQk363Zq3_YerR4ML-cAuEVmqFy2XSA.

[3]I first encountered this story when I was taking a class on the teachings of G. I. Gurdjieff from Cynthia Bourgeault through Spirituality and Practice. The story was printed in the online teachings of Session 2, November 4, 2014.

[4]St. Francis of Assisi, *The Testament of St. Francis,* as translated by Diane M. Houdek in her book, *Lent with St. Francis: Daily Reflections,* Franciscan Media, February, 2017; reprinted at *https://www.franciscanmedia.org/minute-meditations/the-least-of-these-2/.* This same quote is traditionally translated, "What had seemed bitter to me was changed into sweetness of soul and body." See, for instance, https://sacred-texts.com/chr/wosf/wosf09.htm.

[5]Thich Nhat Hanh, *The Miracle of Mindfulness: An Introduction to the Practice of Meditation, Revised Edition,* trans. Mobi Ho (Beacon Press, 1987), 61.

[6]The Book of Job, Chapter 40:4b. My translation.

[7]Thomas R. Kelly, *A Testament of Devotion* (Harper One, 1941), 43.

[8]Joanna Macy and Chris Johnstone, *Active Hope: How to Face the Mess We're in Without Going Crazy* (New World Library, 2012), 178–179.

[9]Ross Gay, *Inciting Joy: Essays* (Algonquin Books of Chapel Hill, 2022), 4.

{ 2 }

Red Thread

Songyuan asked, "Why can't clear-eyed Bodhisattvas sever the red thread?"[1]

When I was in my early thirties, a ragtag group of friends and family assembled weekly in my living room to meditate. Our teacher was a recovering alcoholic and self-identified Sufi who taught us glorious chants. We'd sing and sing and sink into a silence unlike any I'd ever known.

Then, one day, our Sufi announced that he had fallen in love and was giving up meditation for sex. The rest of us decided to keep meeting for meditation, but I pondered our teacher's remarks for a long time. Are sex and meditation not compatible?

His decision brought back the frames of my childhood religious education. Catholic grade school in the sixties didn't particularly support the idea that holiness and physical joy could coexist—or maybe those holy folks who were sexually active just didn't make it into *The Lives of the Saints*. Certainly, the saints extolled by my teachers leaned heavily toward celibacy and virginity.

The problem, of course, was that an education like that can lead you to believe that not just sex but any passionate attachment is suspect.

+++ +++ +++

One of the most clarifying moments of my spiritual life happened about a dozen years ago, when I heard a guru-type mock an old woman for her attachment to some trinkets. A desperately poor Indian widow, she'd brought her dowry—a few small silver charms, her only valuables—to a retreat, where they'd been stolen. The community had responded by collecting money for her, an amount far exceeding the value of her loss. Even with this largesse, she was inconsolable. It was this sorrow that occasioned the teacher's scorn.

That teacher never seemed to understand that those few silver charms were the widow's only tangible connection to her children, husband, and parents, now all dead. Somehow, he missed that it might be appropriate to mourn, at least for a while. I got so angry at his lack of human compassion that I spent the entire afternoon walking and committing myself, over and over again, to love this world and its inhabitants. I kept repeating, "I will not abandon my sisters. I will not abandon my brothers."

That man's take on detachment was not unique: I have run into the same distorted thinking in 12-step meetings, churches, ashrams, and temples. It's understandable, as the possible meanings of "detachment" run the gamut from indifference to even-handedness. But using the concept of detachment to denigrate or ignore someone else's pain and suffering is wrong, no matter how you define it.

This is not about being a flat-lander, a person who thinks that the material world is all there is. We can understand that this world is just a time-space way to experience energy and still commit to living as though this reality matters. The way to the fullness—God or Nirvana or Nothingness or Holy Mystery or whatever you call it—is through life, not around it.

Teresa of Calcutta wanted God to break her heart so completely that the whole world could fall in. The Zen Buddhist Songyuan was certain that clear-eyed Bodhisattvas could never sever the red thread of passionate attachment. Both Mother Teresa and Songyuan knew that passionate attachment is meant to lead us to compassion, that love and joy and life and heartache can unlatch the door that appears to close us off from the Infinite.

+++ +++ +++

On Bonnie Raitt's album *Souls Alike*, she sings a song called "Trinkets." It's a strange little number about being a kid who loves a record by Louis Armstrong, a picture by Vincent Van Gogh, and her dog. I don't know what, if any, religious convictions Bonnie Raitt holds. But in "Trinkets," when the singer comes through the Pearly Gates and is asked by an angel what she wants, she names those three things she loved as a child. Love is all that matters in the end. Bonnie Raitt nails it as well as Mother Teresa and Songyuan.

My answer to the question "What do you want?" would be different than Bonnie Raitt's, although I must admit that any catalog of what I love would include my dog Dolly. (More truthfully, Dolly and all my dear departed dogs.) But what's on the list doesn't really matter. It's having a list that counts. We have to learn what love feels like before we can enact it. We have to start with a firm hold on the red thread.

When I know how it feels to really love—not simply to crave something but to risk being broken wide open—that is the beginning of experiencing Love. Real Love, the kind that longs for the wholeness of the other, that simply appreciates the other as they are, leaves us completely undefended. From that vulnerable place, we can be drawn out of the small self to the far reaches of eternity, into the depth and joy of the Love that moves the sun and other stars. We enter the Divine Mystery even as Divine Mystery beats within our chest.

+++ +++ +++

As for my Sufi teacher, I have come to believe that he never intended to give up his spiritual practice. He simply intended to use the joy of the body and the piercing depth of love as his practice. It's one way to the Holy!

+++   +++   +++

[1]Buddhist oral tradition, cited in John Tarrant, *Bring Me the Rhinoceros and Other Zen Koans to Bring You Joy* (Harmony Books, 2004), 80.

{ 3 }

Cosmic and Particular

Our daughter-in-law, Jane, interprets the saying "It takes a village to raise a child" liberally. Of course, in these days, municipal boundaries are a bit wider than they used to be. A day's plane journey appears to mark the village limits for our family.

Which is why you would have found me in Washington, D.C. soon after Ella arrived.

+++ +++ +++

We had it planned for almost a year, all of us grandparents. After the baby was born, when Jane went back to work, we would each take a turn and move in for a while: a two-to-three-week stint getting to know Ella Rose, helping ease the family into a life that involved two jobs and a new baby. And lucky me—only a step-grandparent, really, but I was welcomed in as if this child were my own blood.

I gotta tell you, it was some grand time I had.

This is how it goes when you fall in love with a baby. There's the nasty task of poopy diapers mingled with joy when she grabs her toes and chortles. There's the weird feeling of a small person farting on your leg and your own delight in her loud belch. There's the smell of a baby's head—oh Lord, that wonderful smell. There's watching her suck so hard that she chokes, calming her when she's beside herself, walking the floor and singing her to sleep, and cleaning spit-up off her face and your clothes. There is the reality of shaping your entire day around the needs of a twelve-pound, God-infested beauty.

In between the baby tasks and the general work of the house, I managed to read *A General Theory of Love* by Lewis, Amini, and Lannon.[1] It's a great book. If you were to pick up my copy, you'd find dog-eared, underlined page after dog-eared, underlined page. As I was learning to attend to this small being, I was simultaneously reading about the profound effect that loving attention has on the open-loop physiology of an infant. It was amazing to read a scientific explanation of what I was experiencing: Because I'd paid attention to the way Ella cried when she was tired, and because I didn't get frustrated or afraid but instead held a calm place in my heart (in the book's parlance, did my own limbic regulation), she could let go, flop against my shoulder, sigh, and slide into sleep. In a new way, I understood just how particular we each need love to be and why we long for someone to "get" us, to notice us as an individual. It's not just a good thing, this kind of specific, attentive love. It is the thing that assures our very survival. It makes us whole.

I also managed, while living in the midst of this very focused love, to view "My Stroke of Insight."[2] In this video from a TED conference, the neuroanatomist Jill Bolte Taylor describes the joy she experienced when she had a stroke, and the left hemisphere of her brain finally shut up. I sat in front of the computer and wept, and then I watched it again, and then I emailed it to George so he could see it too.

And then, since I was in DC, I had to visit one of my favorite museums. I spent a day at the Museum of Natural History, where I stood in the rock section and looked at a tiny vial of stardust, full of infinitesimal diamonds—the same kind of stardust from which the entire cosmos was created.

++ +++ +++

That was my trip: particular, cosmic; cosmic, particular. I flew home thinking about how these two very different and essential realities fit together inside us, how they combine to make us fully human.

I kept on thinking about these things and wondering how to write about them until yesterday afternoon when I looked across the lake.

When I look out the window at my desk, I see the blocky peaks of English Mountain and Mt. Denver. Between them, they cup the New Denver glacier, which, like most all the glaciers across North America, is shrinking. Like most all the glaciers in North America, it will disappear, probably in my lifetime. Unlike all the other glaciers in North America, this one is part of my daily life. Over my computer screen, right now, I can see its top. I love this glacier. When it is gone, I don't know how I will be able to stop crying.

I'll be weeping for more than the New Denver glacier, of course. I'm already weeping for loss of habitat, cyclone victims, diminished and unpredictable water flows, for the human and animal and plant suffering that global climate change is bringing about. But I know and love this particular glacier. It's love of this glacier, this place with its trees and streams and bears and toads, that has propelled me to do more intentional environmental work.

As I looked at the glacier yesterday, it hit me that I believe this is exactly the way that particular love is supposed to move us. Of course, we are supposed to love particular people and specific things. That's what it is to be a human. When Francis Geddes taught me to do healing prayer, he taught me that my first task was to open my heart to the person for whom I'm praying. I know I'm ready to pray when I look at the lines on their face or the shadows under their eyes and feel compassion.[3]

+++ +++ +++

There are some spiritual paths which seem to encourage detachment from joy as well as suffering, but that's not my path. I think that to deny the importance of particular love is to reject human-ness. I do understand the psychological importance of detachment. I just happen to believe that passion is just as important.

After all, passion is a central concept in Christianity—not just the suffering passion of Jesus dying on the cross, but the loving pas-sion that fueled his work of healing and speaking and touching. When I feel deep love and concern, do all that I am capable of doing as is appropriate to a situation, and then let go and acknowledge that it's out of my hands, that's detachment. Detachment is the last step, not the first one. It has to start with passion.

Allowing the particular—my granddaughter Ella, the New Den-ver glacier—to ignite my passion is a good thing, as long as it doesn't stop there. Were I so short-sighted as to only care about the particulars in my immediate life—unable to see the people and places closest to me as icon or cipher for the cosmic whole—then particularity would indeed be a bad idea, sure to get me into fights with the neighbors. Nearsighted particularity inflicts suffering and ignites wars.

But passion, that deep love of the particular, when it is extended and fully realized, has the capacity to draw us out beyond ourselves. We start first by going to the place where we are willing to take risks and make ourselves uncomfortable for those dear to us. Then, we extend that love to those who are dear to others, and finally to that which God holds dear—to all of humanity, to all of the natural world, to the wide cosmic reaches.

There is an instinctual hesitation about loving so deeply, because we are sure to get hurt. Loss too is a reality in the world of the par-ticular. But holding back means that we miss out on the way in which particularity opens us to the big picture, the way in which babies and stardust awaken the cosmic tune in our hearts. Love of this baby can crack me open to other babies, to doing something about famine or abuse or education or the need for a minimum in-come. Love of this glacier can move me to love all glaciers, change my buying and driving habits, and spend my energy on environmental issues.

There's room for the whole world if we just start one baby, one glacier at a time.

+++ +++ +++

[1] Thomas Lewis, Fari Amini, and Richard Lannon, *A General Theory of Love* (Vintage, 2001).

[2] Jill Bolte Taylor, "My Stroke of Insight," TED Talk, February 2008, https://www.ted.com/talks/jill_bolte_taylor_my_stroke_of_insight?subtitle=en

[3] Let me put in a plug here for Francis Geddes, *Contemplative Healing: The Congregation as Healing Community* (iUniverse, 2011). Fran taught a form of healing prayer that was undramatic, deeply grounded in Christianity, and spectacularly open, theologically. He trained hundreds of people on the West Coast of the US to take seriously the invitation to heal each other. Through this work, he changed thousands of lives, mine included, and I bow in gratitude.

{ 4 }

Street Walkers

Eight years ago, in our lake, at the mouth of the bay where we locals swim, four young people drowned. I have not felt like I could tell this story. It is, for some families, a private and forever grief upon which I have no right to intrude.

But parts of that story belong to me and to George. And that's what I want to tell here.

+++ +++ +++

This is how it was for weeks after they died:

We get up early and check in briefly at the school with the counselors and the RCMP liaison. We go downtown. We start walking west on the main street, wondering what to do. It occurs to me to go look at Bigelow Bay, where the divers are trying to recover these children of our village. I turn right at the corner, barely noticing what a lovely day it is. There are streams of people walking either toward the bay or away from it. There are people standing in their front yards. We nod at each other, or stand together silently, or walk in cadence. There's very little speech. What is said comes in whispers.

Sometimes, I catch someone's eye. I hold out my arms, or they hold their arms out to me. We come to each other like children running to their mothers after a hard fall, and I feel for a few long seconds the weight and warmth of another body against my chest, the pulse of a heart beating, the solidity—the life.

Sometimes, someone needs to tell a story, maybe about not being able to look at the lake yet. Or maybe they tell about playing an instrument out over the water at night, or of holding someone who was weeping and how they don't know what to say.

Often, people have something to give. The local chocolatier drives around in her scooter with a full cooler, handing out samples. People keep offering food to other people, organizing meals for distraught extended families, bringing treats to the school, taking dinner to the neighbors. The coffee shop gives out free drinks. Free hugs are everywhere.

Sometimes, people are worried. Has anyone talked to this person who was so upset? Who is taking care of this child? Do you know how we can get some counselling for this family? Do they have enough money? Does that family want people to visit? What can I do to help? Does anyone need a place to stay? It feels like the questions never end.

This is how the days go: George and I walk, and listen, and hold, and make connections.

We walk all day, and at night we sit on the porch with Dolly the dog, looking out over the lake. We eat ice cream.

+++   +++   +++

When I moved here, alone, in the middle of a blizzard, in the middle of January, into a huge house on a hill outside of a village where I knew no one, I lost myself. I like to think it was an intentional loss, planned by an inner wisdom that knew I would never grow if I weren't stripped of my oh-so-comfortable roles. But damn, it was a hard year. I wept every day as I trudged up and down the icy road with the dog. I wept when I sat down to meditation. I wept when I looked at the disappearing glacier. I wept when the cedars were shriveling from the drought.

But mostly, I wept because no one wanted what I had to offer: a deep sense of the abiding and infinite love of Christ.

As the years went on, this last suffering resolved into a kind of dull ache, a knowing that my community was repelled by that which I loved best. I used to say to George, "This place is not only unchurched, it's anti-churched." And I wondered why the hell I was here, and what the hell I was supposed to be doing, and whether I was really a Christian.

+++ +++ +++

When one of my "away" friends heard about our community's horrific loss and how George and I were walking the streets, she said to me, "Oh, they will see Christ in you."

But that wasn't how it was at all. It was like this:

One night on the porch, eating ice cream, George looked over at me with tears streaming down his face and said, "I saw Jesus today. I saw him everywhere."

{ 5 }

Fecundity and Loss

Normally, I have to wait for the dog when we walk up the creek. Normally, she ambles up the road, stopping regularly to sniff (my brother Ed calls it checking her pee-mail) and mark a spot. Normally, I am the one waiting. But last Sunday was different.

It was the end of August. On Saturday evening, the last summer company—family and friends—left. On Monday, the first retreat person was arriving. It was the turning of the year, movement from swimming and laughing into silence and writing. I was in a nostalgic mood already.

It was also one of those days. The wind down the draw was warm, but there was a hint of something else under it—the trace of a smell, a barely perceptible coolness that said autumn was coming. I could see it all around me: The wild black currants were thick on the bushes, the blueberries almost ripe, the huckleberries and thimbleberries wizened, a handful of leaves tinted yellow. So I made my way up the creek grazing on currants, which I shared with Rose, stopping to look and sniff, myself. This time, she waited as I drank in the path at every turn.

All the way up to the bridge, I felt gripped by that mix of loss and excitement that's impossible to pin down. Like Proust's madeleine cookies, it is to be experienced, not held. I savored the present as well as childhood memories of tasting Concord grapes in the neighbor's backyard and peeling off the spiny husk of a horse chestnut to find its silky brown nut. I was struck by the wild fecundity of the world around me, the thousands of seeds ripening, the

sheer volume of the physical world's joy that is expressed in reproduction.

+++ +++ +++

I suppose I was also in a reflective frame of mind because the day
before, August 22nd, was the anniversary of my father's death. With
eight children, he was a solid example of nature's fecundity. The experience came close to breaking him. In my adult years, I have seen
more clearly what a burden he carried and feel deep gratitude for
his commitment to us. I also see more clearly the ways that I resem-
ble him, both in terms of the strains we feel and the things we relish.

One of my more joyful inheritances is his love of wilderness—more specifically, all the edible bits of wilderness. When I
made my way, berries in hand, up the creek to the bridge, I thought
about how much he would have loved this place and how happy he
would have been to know that this is now my home.

That mixture of fecundity and death, munificence and loss, has
been on my mind a lot these days. I suppose it's one way that I deal
with my concern about the physical world and all the ways we humans are destroying it: I try to remember that even if we extermi-
nate ourselves, this natural world has a drive toward exuberant
procreation that will eventually rebalance the planet. Sometimes,
this knowledge is a great comfort. But mostly I feel a deep sadness
that we humans are ruining it for everyone—not just our own
species, but billions of other beings as well. If we are indeed the consciousness of this biosphere, we have a lot of growing up to do, and
quickly. Will it only be through the great losses at the end that we
will find our hearts?

+++ +++ +++

In my meanderings around this question, I've felt drawn into an experiential knowing—not easy to say in words, but I can feel it—of the way that we human beings are part of the cycle of life and death and of how that all fits into the Holy. As a physical self, we decay into mud and water, slide down into the earth. We might be drawn up into a tree or spring up as a turnip or a tomato or a tricholoma. We get incorporated into another human or a voracious deer or another plant and start over. Our material bits never quit being part of the cycle of life, the bursting forth of matter, the flowering of the cosmos. Even rocks have a life cycle, though it's way longer than I can usually hold in view.

As for our spirit parts, our soul, our Self-ness? Well, it seems to me that the spirit bit returns when we die also, but into the Holy Cosmic Soup from whence we came, into the Divine One-ness that is God and Mystery and Balance and Harmony and Justice and Beauty and, above all, Love. From there, who knows? I can taste the sense that I might be able to keep on loving in a specific way, with my own flavor, after my death. But that is a veiled little morsel of knowing requiring blind faith.

+++ +++ +++

This fecundity of the natural, physical world—I can read all the scientific explanations of evolution's drive to assure reproduction, but none of it prepares me for the sheer poetry of bursting pods or burdened branches, the spinning brilliance of clear winter night skies, the gazillion toadlets marching off to hibernation; for the way my heart thumps and sings in the presence of this much much-ness. Nor am I prepared for the grief that comes with each death—from my father to the hemlock with root rot or the skunk by the side of the road.

I suppose that this push and pull, these movements between the poles of joy and loss, are the essence of being human. We are capable of treasuring the numinous, ecstatic experiences as well as the flesh-and-blood realities that tear the heart open. To be human is to know ourselves in situ, part of something not only larger but much more complex and paradoxical. Thomas Merton says this:

> As long as we are on earth the love that unites us will bring us suffering by our very contact with one another. Because of this, love is the resetting a body of broken bones. Even saints cannot live with saints on this earth without some anguish, without some pain at the differences that come between them.[1]

I'd like to note that it's not just humans who are part of this unity and exchange. We can't live in the physical world of animals and plants and rocks and water without engendering and experiencing suffering. We're invited to mend things there, too—that's what love of the natural world means. As with purely human relationships, this is an impossible task which will break our hearts.

Lucky us, to come to the world with hearts broken open. Everything falls into an open heart. That's fullness. That's fecundity.

+++ +++ +++

[1] Thomas Merton, *New Seeds of Contemplation* (New Directions, 1961), 72.

{ 6 }

Time to Give It All Away

There's a new mental disorder stalking the Western world: Nature Deficit Disorder.[1] Our widespread disconnection from the natural world—most of us can't distinguish one tree from another, don't walk in the woods, don't look at the stars, rarely stand in an unaltered landscape—is making us sick. The list of effects I found in the official diagnosis includes depression, limited attention span, stress, obesity, and even myopia.

Well, I'm gravely myopic. I admit to a touch of extra weight, a limited attention span, possibly a soupçon of mania. And stress? You would feel it too if you had to deal with what I had to deal with this fall: full-on and flat-out abundance.

Currently awaiting attention in the garage are green tomatoes ripening under cover, plum vinegar in need of decanting, and three boxes of apples waiting to be sauced, pied, or chutney-ed. Already on the storage shelves are jars of salsa, raspberry jam, plum sauce, cherry vinegar, and black currant jelly. There are thirty quarts of apple cider, too, along with garlic, onions, and squash. In the basement, you'll find potatoes, while the back-porch freezer holds pesto, dried tomatoes, tomato sauce, bags of blueberries and raspberries, and plums and apples cut for pie. The pantry contains dried apples and plums, and I can't count the boxes and bags of fresh produce that have gone to good homes since July.

I am not a great gardener. Nor am I a food-security junkie. This orgy of picking, slicing, pickling, drying, juicing, fermenting, saucing, jellying, and freezing was simply a response to the outrageous bounty of our garden and orchard.

All fall, I puzzled over my feverish preservation of food. What motivated this behavior? The facile answer was that I hate to waste anything. The deeper answer lay in the weather.

+++ +++ +++

When I started reading climate projections years ago, I couldn't imagine how they would touch my daily life. But like millions across the world, we have not simply been touched, we have been walloped. We're sitting in front-row seats for global climate change. The world is groaning, trying to adapt to the strains and stresses we've introduced. Like an animal senseless in its pain, it is lashing back.

Our personal version of the worldwide distress was a smoke-choked summer spent on evacuation alert. Even now, in December, this inland rain forest is struggling with the aftermath of outrageous summer heat and an ongoing drought. Of course, this is a minor inconvenience when compared to other parts of the world. Flood, fire, famine; air pollution, earthquake, hurricane, scorching heat: It feels as if nature has gone rogue in a whirl of intemperate activity.

If you are brave, listen to the weather reports whenever a new storm is arriving somewhere. The endless catalogue of the horrors ahead is intended to tell us that we should be afraid, very afraid.

It breaks my heart, this dread we are cultivating. It's no wonder we suffer from Nature Deficit Disorder. How can we love when we are drowning in fear? Why bother learning about types of trees when they're all going to die anyway?

But loving or not loving is a choice, albeit a difficult choice when you're shaking with fright. Here is the place where I decided to start: I am going to love this earth enough to witness its generosity. I will thank each and every tree and plant that bloomed and fruited, every drop of rain that came when it was needed, the immense effort expended to keep life on track. I will celebrate with wonder, awe, and gratitude the planet's commitment to fecundity.

Remember that, in the midst of its own dislocation and injuries, this living world still provides for its constituents.

+++ +++ +++

I have made two other choices as a way of dealing with my distress and foreboding: curiosity and trust. When I got curious about why this was such a productive year, I learned that when a tree reproduces with vast abundance, it is more likely a desperate attempt to keep the species alive rather than a sign of health. You could say that the wealth of my pantry came from plants and trees who were stressed. This knowledge kindled a gut-felt kinship for the scrawny old tree in the front yard whose gaunt branches birthed boxes and boxes of deep purple plums. That plum tree shows me that anxiety is not a reason to quit. Instead, it's a cue, telling me that now is the time to give it all away.

Finally, there is trust. This is not trust that everything will get better in my lifetime, but trust that I have a part to play in the healing of the world, whatever that healing might look like. I can trust that I am a particular and necessary part of the solution, not simply a nasty parasite.

I am trying to keep firmly in mind and heart that my small mortal life is to be spent in the service of life here on the blue-green mystery in which we live and move and have our being. Like that ancient plum tree, the goal is to ripen all the fruit I can. My aspiration: to give it all away.

+++ +++ +++

[1]Nature Deficit Disorder is a term coined by the journalist and author Richard Louv and reported on in such publications as *Psychology Today*. Louv's work has been recognized by the Audubon Society, the American Academy of Pediatrics, the White House

Summit on Environmental Education, and others. However, Nature Deficit Disorder is not recognized in medical manuals (e.g., DSM-5) as a mental disorder.

PART II: I PLACE THEM ON WHAT IS BEAUTIFUL

{ 7 }

On the Edge of a Grimpen

On the edge of a grimpen, where is no secure foothold,
And menaced by monsters.
T.S. Elliott, "East Coker," *Four Quartets*

At a recent monthly board meeting of our local lake stewardship society, a friend began waxing poetic about the wetlands of our area. These moist and messy places are the most biologically diverse spots on earth, she claimed. She named wetlands as the lungs and kidneys of the planet's watersheds: essential, irreplaceable. Plus, she added, they prevent flooding.

But she didn't stop there. She said that our wetlands, the ones in this valley, are unique. Because dams destroy the natural wetlands on lakes and rivers, and because the Slocan is the only un-dammed watershed in the Columbia River system, our area constitutes a template for restoration attempts across the Columbia Basin.

After all this, she made a pitch for us to sponsor a wetlands workshop and then to join a loose affiliation whose purpose would be to assess and map wetlands.

I voted in favor of these suggestions, grudgingly and with trepidation. While I understand the importance of mucky places, I find it hard to love a wetland. In fact, they horrify me.

+++ +++ +++

I blame my fears on the stories told by my brothers when I was three, prior to a family move from the shores of Puget Sound to rural Georgia. In those tales—whispered in the dark when the parents weren't listening—sucking mud and snapping alligators were prominent. My trepidation might have sunk into simple unease were it not for the fact that the actual experience of rural Georgia did indeed encompass alligators and viscous sludge. It also included swimming holes infested with water moccasins; woods overrun with rattlesnakes, chiggers, and ticks; and swamps populated with leeches and carnivorous plants. I am still unable to walk among high grasses without a frisson of terror, while a boggy patch in the trail makes me leap for hummocks. Although I appreciate the concept of wetlands, I don't really want one close to me.

I don't think I'm alone in my ambivalence about swampy places. The province is currently engaging in something that looks familiarly equivocal, as one agency allows developers to fill in the flyway marshes south of Vancouver (more shopping malls and condos, hooray!), while another funds the construction of artificial sloughs to prevent flooding.

+++ +++ +++

This might have simply developed into a short treatise on the magnificence of the hydrological cycle if it hadn't occurred to me that there's an internal match for my external dislike. I probably fear those inner mucky places more deeply than any waterlogged ground on which I've trod.

In my experience, internal wetlands are scary places for exactly the same reason that external wetlands are scary places: They teem with life, but not necessarily benevolent life. As a friend said recently, "That stuff in there can kill you." It feels, when I get into one of these mucky inner spaces, as if a single wrong step could plant me in quicksand. At the very least, internal swamps render me uncertain of my direction, prey to all sorts of bloodsuckers, wet—as in tearful--and conspicuously sullied.

These days, I've been reading and rereading the essay "Suffering" from Helen Luke. It's probably the most succinct, thoughtful, and deeply spiritual work I've ever read on human suffering. I've been reading and rereading it because I got stuck in some stupid suffering this year. In a series of curiously similar interactions where I was working hard to be gracious in a difficult situation, the other person involved accused me of being profoundly uncaring. Because none of these conversations were private, not only did I feel misjudged, I also felt publicly humiliated. Although I held my temper, I can tell you that the next stop in my mind was anger and indignation. All in all, I was handed a sure ticket to a nasty inner quagmire.

(An aside: There's something about the claim that I was working hard to be gracious that smacks of pomposity, isn't there? I'm leaving those words, as distasteful as they are, to remind me of how blind I can be to my own shit.)

Anyway. Luke, who was a Jungian psychotherapist, stressed that there are two kinds of suffering. There's "real" suffering, and something else which she labeled "neurotic" suffering—that guilt-laden, self-focused suffering where we go around and around the same territory. I did this neurotic thing for a while. I obsessively revisited the specifics of those uncomfortable events. I would think of how wrong the other person was and get angry, then I'd think about where I'd screwed up and feel shame. Then I'd get to thinking of what I should have said, remembering what the person had done to me in the past, and get mad all over again. Tears, bloodsuckers, and lost bearings, indeed.

+++ +++ +++

If I were being truthful, I'd admit that my preferred way of dealing with an inner quagmire isn't neurotic suffering. I instinctually opt to avoid the issue altogether, pretending that the mess doesn't exist. But that kind of denial requires that I perform the emotional equivalent of dumping truckloads of sand and gravel (i.e., sweets, novels, busyness) over the top of the muck in an attempt to find something, anything, that will take that discomfort away.

Maybe this would be fine if it actually worked, but it doesn't. The internal landscape really does mirror the external world here. Anyone who has attempted to fill a wetland knows that more fill is required than you can possibly imagine. Then, after you've used the whole damn gravel pit, you've got a lifeless spot of land subject to flash floods and sinkholes. Only now it's all the more dangerous because the problem has been covered over. It's sort of like when I do a really thorough job on denial, and I don't even know I'm in pain.

Helen Luke is pretty harsh about this kind of avoidance. She puts it so clearly when she writes, "Deeply ingrained in the infantile psyche is the conscious or unconscious assumption that the cure for depression is to replace it with pleasant happy feelings, whereas the only valid cure for any kind of depression lies in the acceptance of real suffering."[1]

Real suffering is something entirely different from neurotic suffering or denial. Luke says that real suffering consists of consciously picking up and carrying our humiliation without any attempt to self-justify. We're not resisting, judging, or angry, nor are we resigned, coerced, or giving up. We simply are present to what hurts, without resistance and without defeat. Suffering is about innocence, she says, not about guilt and ego-centered shame.

+++ +++ +++

So I've been trying to be present to the suffering lately, and I'm making a little bit of headway, enough to imagine how the other person may have felt in one of these sticky situations, enough to admit the ambiguity of my own behavior, enough to imagine meeting the other again with love in my heart. I've even tried to objectively accept my own guilt and shame and simply let myself be pierced. But there still seemed to be a piece missing, a part of the toolkit that I wasn't getting.

Everything finally came together about two weeks ago. I was headed to Spokane to pick up a retreat leader, and I decided to listen to an old CD from Cynthia Bourgeault while I drove.[2] Curiously, she was dealing with this same reading from Helen Luke. She added, however, the description of how it feels inside of us when we allow real suffering: We refrain from bracing. "Keep your inner core feeling open and vulnerable," she said. Not helpless—that coils down into anger—but open in that way that has curiosity and steadiness mixed in.

When I heard this, I decided to practice it right away. I needed to because, as usual, I was running late and feeling anxious. But the world gave me a much bigger opportunity for practice than I'd hoped for.

I'd picked up our presenter, and we were trying to make it home for a late dinner. Then we hit the border, where things went sideways. When the border guard asked my guest the purpose of his trip, and I said, "Oh, he's coming to lead a retreat for us" at the same time that he said, "I'm just coming to visit friends," she got suspicious. It was hard to know how to answer some of the questions she asked, and everything we said seemed wrong. The guard accused our guest of trying to work without a permit (he didn't need one). I was repeatedly asked if I was bringing in drugs or alcohol. The car was searched. We were both accused of providing false information.

I had several different reactions during this extended event, and they cycled through regularly. The first encompassed anger and blame: How dare she treat me like this? Why did he say that? Why is he growing that stupid beard? The second was shame: Why did I say that? I shouldn't have said that. How stupid am I? He's gonna hate me. Then there was the third reaction, the one I worked to come back to over and over again: Don't brace. Stay soft inside. Just stay here and don't judge her or him or yourself.

When, an hour and a half later, we were told that we were free to leave, I was tired and hungry. Surprisingly, I wasn't angry. (I can't quite say that I wasn't resentful, since this story still carries enough charge for me to remember it, but heck, I was not very resentful, anyway.) I realized that I'd felt compassion for all the players in that little drama even as it was happening. Most surprising to me was that I had no idea how long we had been there. I thought it was twenty minutes.

I am not going to pretend that this was a good time. It was an honest-to-God swamp, dammit. It felt dangerous. I wanted to cry, I was confused, I had no idea whether something really bad was going to happen, and I definitely wasn't in control. But I don't think that I added to the suffering inherent in the situation—not my own suffering, not my guest's suffering, not even the suffering of the border guard. I just worked to carry the part of it that was mine. So that worked, I guess—that practice of not bracing on the inside.

+++ +++ +++

I hope it's clear that the inward moves I'm describing are not intended to simply benefit myself, like some private system of water filtration. Instead, when I am willing to enter my inner wetland, I acknowledge my place in the cosmic ecosystem. Metaphorically, my fen and your bog interact. Here is the way I understand it, courtesy of a basic lesson in hydrology:

When a wetland is destroyed, a domino effect commences because the water that used to be filtered in that wetland still needs someplace to go. So the water causes great slides of mud or runs off to flood the adjacent areas or tears downhill at high speed, causing deep and undermining channels. A "decommissioned" wetland no longer deals with its own problems. Instead, it shoves them off on the neighbors.

This is exactly what Helen Luke says about suffering. Our choice to bear our own suffering has an impact on others:

> Every time a person exchanges neurotic depression for real suffering, he or she is sharing to some small degree in the carrying of the suffering of mankind, in bearing a tiny part of the darkness of the world... The smallest consent to the fierce, sharp pain of objective suffering in the most trivial-seeming matter may have an influence, as the Chinese sage puts it, "at a distance of a thousand miles."[3]

When I choose to carry the suffering that is really mine, then no one else has to be burdened with it. If my swamp is filtering groundwater as it should, the runoff won't drown someone else. It's not the act of a martyr or an attempt to fix myself or you. Carrying my own suffering is a simple act of humility. We cease to fight what is.

I know now that when I allow—however haltingly—that fierce, sharp pain, I also allow the experience of myself as part of the whole, one in the One. Like the wetlands in the hills around us, if I can take in what's mine, the death-dealing bits will filter out and sink into a rich compost. Then I'll be in a position to make gentle offerings: water of life for our human relations, water of life for our planet.

+++ +++ +++

[1]Helen Luke, "Suffering," in *Old Age: Journey into Simplicity* (Parabola, 1987), 104.

[2]Cynthia Bourgeault, "An Introduction to Centering Prayer," produced by and STILL available from The Contemplative Society,

2017, https://www.contemplative.org/product/an-introduction-to-
the-practice-of-centering-prayer/.

[3]Luke, "Suffering," 107–108.

{ 8 }

Genevieve at the Gates of Heaven

Genevieve arrived just before my forty-sixth birthday. She was the first dog George and I had ever owned, and we'd both fallen in love immediately with this middle-aged beagle who'd been found wandering the streets of Chualar, California. It appeared that she was just what we wanted in a pet: affectionate, smart, mannerly, and low maintenance.

Well, scratch low maintenance. A week after she came home with us, we discovered that Genevieve had severe diabetes. This meant a special diet, daily insulin injections, two different dietary supplements, and weekly vet visits. Then, a month later, she was diagnosed with diabetic cataracts, necessitating immediate and very costly eye surgery—or she would become blind within weeks. It seemed unfair to expect her to adjust to a new life without sight, so our entire tax rebate, which was supposed to go into savings, got handed over to the veterinary surgeon. Can you tell how much we loved this dog already?

+++ +++ +++

Fast forward to the summer. We were hiking down a trail in Big Sur toward the ocean. This was a riding as well as walking path, and there were a few places where we had to step carefully to avoid the piles of horse manure. But nothing could spoil our pleasure. It was a beautiful and temperate day. Genevieve was delighted to be off leash. Her eyes were healed, and we had stabilized her diabetes. We were the picture of a happy family: a healthy, nice-looking dog trotting obediently between two healthy, nice-looking humans toward the beach. At least, that was the picture—until Genevieve decided that she wanted to sample road apples.

By the time we noticed what she was doing, she had her mouth full of horseshit and was not interested in letting go. George and I knelt in the path, one on each side, trying to pry open her stubborn little jaw. She tried just as hard to keep her teeth clamped shut around her prize. My concern wasn't so much about hygiene, though that certainly entered my mind. What I kept worrying about was how horse manure would affect her blood sugar.

We pleaded. We bribed her with treats. We yelled. We stuck our fingers in her mouth to pry it open. We attempted to reach in and flick out the shit. While she did her pigheaded best to keep her treasure safe, we acted like anxious, incompetent humans, trying ineffectual intervention after ineffectual intervention.

In the end, we gave up.

+++ +++ +++

As I leaned back on my heels in the middle of the trail—easing down, naturally, into a pile of manure—a sudden image came to mind. I saw myself as Genevieve, jaws clenched, tenaciously holding on to something that was going to make me sick. How many times had the Holy invited me to let go of something that was not conducive to my spiritual or physical health? How many times had I sensed an inner voice saying, "Darling, that really is going to make you feel terrible," only to respond by closing my mouth more firmly around the thing I wanted? How many times had I insisted that yes, I really did want to eat this shit?

+++ +++ +++

At that moment, I was seized by a sense of overwhelming joy and boundless compassion. It was like the gates of heaven opening, trumpets sounding. I couldn't stop laughing. I knew that I didn't want to punish Genevieve, not by a long shot. I just wanted to help her because I loved her so unreservedly. I would grieve if she got sick, and wish that she had made a better choice, and love her madly anyway. How could the Divine be any less loving toward me? I felt bathed in love. And the possibility that I didn't have to punish myself for those bad and harmful choices, that I could love myself in all my flaws...? Well, it felt possible.

{ 9 }

Pretty New Bag

Friday, exactly two weeks ago, I stopped by my friend DJ's store. I was leaving town the next day for a long-awaited retreat and wanted to check with her about some details for an upcoming gathering.

I could have called her, but I didn't—because, you see, there was something in that store that I'd been eyeing for a long time.

DJ carries all kinds of beautiful, locally made things. You can find pottery, jewelry, sweet little booties and mittens and scarves, gorgeous photos and cards—and bags. Big leather shoulder bags made by a Coast Salish elder, a woman who cuts up cast-off leather garments and puts them back together in lovely huge purses covered with traditional designs. She layers these patchwork designs over a sturdy backing material so that the old really is capable of maintaining its new beauty.

I had been looking at one bag for close to a year. Serviceable, colorful, it had lots of pockets inside, and on the front was Raven with the sun in his beak. I'd fingered this pouch, tried it on, admired it, and attempted to convince my friends to buy it, but still it hung there. It was just a bit too expensive and too unnecessary to justify.

On that Friday, I snapped. I told myself that I really needed something that could carry both my computer and my purse-things for traveling. Yes, I had a black briefcase that George had handed down to me a number of years ago, but it's just not a pretty thing at all, and I do like pretty things.

So, despite the balance of our bank account, I took that bag down, wrote a check, and carried it home. And the next day I carried it out of the house with my passport in the nice little flapped back pocket, my wallet in the inner compartment, my boarding passes and itinerary tucked into side flaps, and my computer and a book slipped neatly into the main pocket. It was beautiful and tidy, and I felt like I was good to go.

+++ +++ ++

I signed up for this retreat more than a year ago. I'd been voraciously reading the books of Cynthia Bourgeault—the retreat leader—for the past eighteen months and really wanted to connect with her and the community that supports her. She speaks of the human experience with such grace and honesty that it takes my breath away. Here she is, writing about incarnation and the inevitable constriction, suffering, and restraint we experience:

> Could it be that this earthly realm, not in spite of but because of its very density and jagged edges, offers precisely the conditions for the expression of certain aspects of divine love that could become real in no other way? This world does indeed show forth what love is like in a particularly intense and costly way. But when we look at this process more deeply, we can see that those sharp edges we experience as constriction at the same time call forth some of the most exquisite dimensions of love, which require the condition of finitude in order to make sense—qualities such as steadfastness, tenderness, commitment, forbearance, fidelity, and forgiveness. These mature and subtle flavors of love have no real context in a realm where there are no edges and boundaries, where all just flows. But when you run up against the hard edge and have to stand true to love anyway, what emerges is a most precious taste of pure divine love. God has spoken his most intimate name.[1]

So, you can guess what I encountered. Indeed, Cynthia Bourgeault was all I had hoped for: wise, deep, openhearted, brilliant. Her contemplative cosmology—which incorporated quantum physics—resonated deeply with my own experience. Her treatment of the suffering and beauty of incarnation was inspirational. My fellow retreatants were generous and thoughtful; the Tucson desert was beautiful; the rooms and food were great; and there was a perfect blend of meditation and chanting, intellectual work, silence, and the practice of presence during physical work.

Even with a head cold and a norovirus outbreak (the first time I've ever meditated through throwing up), it was a remarkable experience. I felt like I was able to own the depths of Christianity thoroughly and integrate it with the science that is changing our worldview. My beloved tradition felt cleansed and reworked, a new and vibrant vessel that could contain both heart and mind. Like my pretty new bag made by that First Nations elder, Cynthia used the old stories, added a sturdy new underlay of contemporary science, and fashioned something beautiful, strong, and functional.

The most difficult part of the retreat was, as always, the internal work. With all that quiet, there was plenty of space to hear my mind's nonstop neurotic commentary. I kept running into those hard edges and boundaries. I judged myself. I judged others. I was embarrassed by saying something stupid. I was jealous. I almost drowned in a sea of wanting: to be part of the inner group, to be special, to say something smart, to get approval. After swatting this stuff away repeatedly for a few days—banging up against those edges—I finally wrote in my journal, *I am bored with myself and my desires.* This exhaustion with the inner drama was a start, at least, toward accepting my complete and often unattractive self so I could find real quiet—and maybe, possibly, a step toward a taste of love, real love; a step toward the capacity to run up against hard edges in the outer world and hold on—with steadfastness, tenderness, commitment, forbearance, fidelity, and forgiveness—those mature and subtle flavors of love.

+++ +++ +++

Wonderful as the retreat was, I have to admit it was a bedraggled and puny version of myself that crawled onto the 6 a.m. flight home a week later. The norovirus had left me weak and unable to eat much, and the head cold was coming on full force. I had managed to find Kleenex, cough drops, cough syrup, sanitary hand-wipes, and reading material to carry along on the plane. But it all caused my lovely raven bag to take on a decidedly lumpen character, with various medical sundries jammed in corners, charge slips hanging out of my wallet, a journal and two novels spilling out of the top. I was grateful to find my seat and room in the overhead bin to stow the whole mess.

The flight was full. Since United charges baggage fees, most people were dragging their luggage with them. I was seated and resting when a youngish woman came storming angrily down the aisle, trying to find room for her suitcase. She attempted to jam it into one bin, where it wouldn't fit because of a seam; yanked it out; and walked back to my row. Looking over my head, she exclaimed loudly, "I don't understand why people think they can put their purses up here," and stormed on.

It took me a minute before I realized she was talking about me. Then I thought, *That's not a purse, it's my computer case. I have a right to put it up there.* Next, I thought, *I paid to check my luggage, she should have too.* Finally came the thought, *Well, this can be a lesson to her about what she gets back when she puts so much anger into the universe.*

Soon after, an elderly Hispanic man showed up who needed to get into the middle seat of my row. He was carrying a duffel bag. At this point I stood up, grabbed my belongings out of the storage bin, and invited him to put his bag up there. Feeling virtuous, I placed my things under the forward seat (Oh! My lovely bag on the nasty plane floor!) and resumed my place.

I was able to feel virtuous for a little while, which was nice, at least until my conscience kicked my ass. You could say that I recognized that I'd backed away, fast, from a hard edge.

+++ +++ +++

I talked to George about it later, saying, "If I had gotten up and offered to move my bag, that woman might have had an entirely different day." He wisely pointed out that my assumption probably wasn't true. It's more likely that she would have felt she'd appropriately made her point and won. *Ah*, I thought. *So, moving the bag to make her "feel better" or change her would have been trying to control or fix her behavior.*

But it still felt like I should have moved my bag, and I finally figured out why.

Because I could. I should have moved my bag because I could. I didn't need her to be right, virtuous, or deserving. It didn't depend on her worthiness or her capacity to change her behavior. She didn't need to be good for me to be nice to her. I could have easily moved the bag. Instead, I chose to do that for someone else, someone to whom it was easier to be kind.

I expect some of you may disagree with me, and that's okay. Maybe you think moving my bag would have been giving in to a bully. But I want to throw out the idea of worthiness, because I'm just plain tired of making judgments about people, myself included. By this, I don't mean that I have quit thinking or that I shouldn't exercise my judgment. I just mean that I am sick of the judgmental sorting that carries on like a background hum through my every waking hour.

Then, too, there's the gospel (Luke 6:27–32): "I say to you, love your enemies, do good to those who hate you... Give to everyone who begs from you; and of him who takes away your goods do not ask them again... For if you love those who love you, what credit is that to you?"

If I am serious about standing true to love at the hard edges, about trying to embody love in this costly, constricted world, then I have to do it without regard for the merit of the person who receives. I don't think I will be able to do this very well. Actually, I know I do it badly and that my behavior isn't likely to change much. It's just human to want to be nice to the ones who are nice to us. But it's those nasty, rude buggers who bang around and make everyone miserable who really need love and consideration. (Okay, they also need to be called to account. But with love and consideration!)

I think I have to make this effort (oh hell!) because otherwise, I may have a pretty new bag, but it's still stuffed with the same old shit.

+++ +++ +++

[1]Cynthia Bourgeault, *The Wisdom Jesus: Transforming Heart and Mind—A New Perspective on Christ and His Message* (Shambhala: 2008), 99–100.

{ 10 }

The Soft Animal

...let the soft animal of your body
love what it loves.
Mary Oliver, "Wild Geese"

When I was in seminary, I had a spiritual director who was also a bodyworker. She always began our sessions by giving me a massage—after all, this was Berkeley in the 1990s. One memorable day, she said, "Therese, your body is so strong. Have you considered what you will do when something stops working, when you find yourself weak?"

I didn't particularly want to get her point. I loved it that I could lift huge pots in the seminary kitchen where I worked, that I could run for miles in the Berkeley hills. I was tough and lean, and it felt great. I figured that if I kept on doing what I was doing, my body would be like that forever.

I haven't been strong forever, of course. The natural processes of life and occasional injuries have changed tough and lean to somewhat gimped and partially pudding-like. But throughout menopause and a broken arm, allergic reactions and shoulder injuries, I always had my strong legs—at least until a few months ago, when my left knee made a noise like a popgun and flowered out in pain.

+++ +++ +++

I am now well acquainted with two physiotherapists and an orthopedic surgeon. Both physiotherapists tell me that the deepest muscles in my leg and torso don't work correctly. The muscles are weak. More importantly, they do not activate properly. I've learned that early injuries can cause the outer muscles, which are all about power, to take over from the inner muscles, which are all about stability.

In other words, my core is unstable.

I have been maintaining my uprightness in an infelicitous and unhealthy manner.

My physiotherapists assigned me a growing list of exercises, each more excruciating than the last. To the naked eye, I might look like I am sitting on the chair relaxing. But in reality, I am tightening my transverse abdominus and oblique muscles while relaxing my rectus abdominus while tightening my gluteus maximus to slightly less than 25 percent—without, of course, arching my back or contracting my shoulders. You try it and see if it doesn't make your head ache. See if the sweat doesn't break out on your brow.

These exercises are also hard because I am not good at them. My physio says that doesn't matter. I should just keep on doing them.

+++ +++ +++

As you might guess, I have been pondering all this. It seems pretty clear that some part of this recent injury—and my general instability—has to do with my unwillingness to attend to my physical self.

Bodies are tricky in this culture. On the one hand, there is a bizarre collective worship of physical beauty and youthfulness. In the throes of our devotion, we go to the gym, spend millions on "product," and undergo physical suffering and surgery to needle on (or off) tattoos, increase (or decrease) our cup size, remove (or add) hair, suck out cellulite, reshape our noses, remove layers of skin, poison our muscles so our faces won't wrinkle, and just plain look like someone who hasn't had our life.

On the other hand, this headlong rush to conform to cultural standards is matched by an equal and opposite "Oh, fuck it" resistance movement. My personal version of this consists of collapsing onto the couch with chocolate and reading for three days straight. Often, my resistance movement is accompanied by feeling ill, since sickness is one of the few ways that I can justify taking time off. While this response can be lovely in small doses, it loses its charm quickly, degenerating into mindlessness and lassitude.

I am not saying that exercise, skin cream, hair color, or vegetation time on the couch are bad ideas. Far from it! But both these poles of behavior treat the body as an object: something to discipline or to placate. This antagonistic stance holds true whether the focus is on outer beauty or inner health. The size of my gut, the skin cancer on my arm, the hairs under my chin, that tricky knee—we all have a list detailing the battles we fight. It's war, not a loving relationship. Speaking for myself, I don't often treat my body as home, beloved self, a gift inseparable from "me."

If I am truthful, I will admit that I almost never neglect to fix my hair (for the sake of appearing socially acceptable) but I don't always take the time to do my exercises. This is in spite of the supposed centrality of incarnation in my worldview, the concept that all physical reality is infused with and inseparable from the Holy. Frankly, it's easier for me to imagine God in the reality of a black bear or a trembling aspen than in this sorry flesh.

+++ +++ +++

Part of what I have tried to face up to in the past few months is that I do not actually pay attention to most of the feedback that my body gives me. Oh, maybe when it says, *I want chocolate*, I listen up, or when I start nodding off over my book in the evening. But I am stone-cold deaf when the message is about discomfort. I can't tell you the number of times I have stood in the kitchen with my back or hip or knee aching and decided to plow ahead rather than take a short rest. Of course, it was this habit of ignoring pain that birthed the serious injury of this spring.

I realized a few weeks ago that I have gotten so used to ignoring aches and throbs that I can no longer tell when I should work through something or when I should stop. I need a professional, for God's sake, to tell me if my leg hurts too much to hike. This is crazy. This is disconnected.

So, my work is slow, these days. My spiritual director suggested that I consider the hour or so I spend each day doing my physio as my spiritual practice. In the same way that meditation practice asks me to stay present, my exercises ask for exquisite awareness of the muscles, joints, and bones of my body. When I let my attention slack off, I usually end up hurting myself.

+++ +++ +++

I've just finished taking a month off work after knee surgery. (I know, from some people's point of view, I don't really work. I have an idyllic life with no set commitments. But that's not what it feels like on the inside, where the inner slave-driver reigns.) This month has been a spiritual effort as gut-churning as the muscle isolations in my belly. I am facing, once again and more deeply, the fact that I tend to maintain my spiritual, as well as my physical, uprightness in an infelicitous and unhealthy manner. That is, I think that my wor-thiness—my right to exist—is the result of my effort, rather than an inherent gift of the Holy Ultimate. Unlike the bear or the quaking aspen, I have to prove I'm okay.

When I heard my physio say, "An old injury that is not properly healed can mean that you are using the wrong muscles to stabilize yourself," my ears perked up. I thought, *That's true about more than just my physical self.*

I know that wounds of trust set all of us up for instability. I know that the natural processes of life—relationship injuries, fear, loss—impel us to stitch together a fabricated self-image in order to stay safe. I know that the social world tells us that the outside—the effigy we want the world to see, whether it's a beautiful physical body or a holy demeanor—is the "real" me. But all of these are as false as the idea that if my power muscles work hard enough, they will become core muscles.

The "real" me is not my harassed ego-self, but the depth of who I am in Love. The "real" me is the belovedness of creation come to fruition in this body, this mind, this heart. My "real" Self can't be created, as it's already been given. It is that place/state/part where the Infinite Holy and my particularity overlap. My particularity is the flavor that this body and this mind and this heart impart to the original gift given by the Love that Pulses at the Center of Everything. I can't earn my Self or create it, only learn to recognize it, honor it, and dwell in it.

So right now—since I'm trying to live out of the place where I don't have to earn anything or impress anyone—my spiritual practice entails exercises, meditation, and attending to my body. I am learning to lie down when I am tired, take time to ice my knee when I don't feel like I have time, walk slowly and deliberately, and ask for—and accept—help.

My spiritual practice also includes forgiving myself for lacking the capacity to plant or tend the garden, forgiving myself for lacking the capacity to listen or tend to others, forgiving myself when I overdo it and my knee swells up or my back goes out, and forgiving myself when I am too tired to think and just want a nap.

In the words of Mary Oliver, I am learning to let the soft animal of my body love what it loves. I am learning to take my place in the family of things.

Do I need to say that I am not good at this practice, either? But, like my difficulty with tightening that transverse abdominus, this lack of skill is ultimately immaterial. What counts is that I practice.

{ 11 }

Embodiment

A couple of years ago, George had a loop recorder—a medical device about the size of a large thumb drive—planted in his chest. The general idea was that this thing would record what happened to his heart during his weird fainting spells so that the doctors could figure out what was going on and how to treat it. After more than a year of tests and questions, it seemed to both of us like a good idea to try this next step.

The process began, like most medical care in a rural area, with the drive—five hours to Kelowna. Once there, a surgeon slit George's chest open, after which he inserted his fingers under George's skin, prying it away from the underlying tissue to make a pocket. Into the pocket he inserted the recorder and then sewed him up. The whole operation was very like what I do to a chicken with garlic cloves, except that the chicken is not alive and talking. But it's very much like a chicken in that if you don't remember that the garlic will make a bulge in the skin, you might make the pocket too small. Hence, what was supposed to be a surgical insertion turned out to be more of a shoving and stuffing. When I do this to poultry, it is usually past caring. Unfortunately, George's local anesthetic ended up being a bit too localized for sufficient detachment.

I was sitting just outside the exam room, listening to all of this. It took about an hour, during which the woman on a gurney a few feet away moaned constantly as she recovered from surgery.

Between the driving, the moaning, the slitting, and the stuffing, the whole experience felt just a bit too embodied. I can't tell you how glad I was when we ate some dinner, downed some drugs (Tylenol 3 for George, chocolate for me), and crawled into our hotel bed. I think we were both asleep before eight o'clock that night.

+++ +++ +++

When I do spiritual direction, I emphasize learning to trust the gut reaction, the flash of intuition. I encourage people to listen to the still, small voice that speaks through the tightness of the chest, the roiling of the stomach, the little headache just behind the eyes. Embodiment isn't some airy-fairy new-age spiritual concept. It's the frank recognition that the physical body knows things that the mind sometimes can't or doesn't want to know. The Holy speaks through the flesh, if we just listen. But the downside of embodiment is—well, it's just so inescapably physical. The limitations and humiliations of the flesh are multiple.

We learned that lesson again the next day, when we returned to the clinic to learn how and when to activate the loop recorder manually. The technician was a youngish woman, both informative and officious. The patronizing edge to her instructions aroused a rage in me that is still not extinguished. I kept wanting to scream, "Do you have any idea who you're talking to?" (When I complained about this experience later at the church potluck, I heard from my elders that they are regularly treated as if they were mentally defective rather than just old. I recognized with a slap that I treat them that way too.)

Of course, it was quite a bit later when I realized how we'd loaded all our pain and fear and frustration from the surgery into this difficult encounter. Poor young woman.

Embodiment. In addition to the joy of the carnal and the wisdom of the flesh, there are the insults to the meat.

+++ +++ +++

It is the joy and the horror of the Christian story that the Holy, the Infinite, the Love at the Center of the Universe, the God-as-you-understand-God, experiences the finite life of the flesh. Christmas traditions show Christ as the child of powerless, impoverished refugees. As best we know, he came to adulthood as a manual laborer in an occupied country. When the gospels catch up with him, he's itinerant and penniless—and certain of God's presence within him. Yet there is no record of him ever screaming, "Do you have any idea who you're talking to?"

Never does he reject the realities of embodiment. His divinity does not cancel out his humanity. Maybe he could have asked for one of those "Get Out of Jail Free" passes so he could skip by the insults of the physical life. He didn't. Instead, he freely chose the human reality—not out of some misguided martyrdom but as an inescapable part of the path. His life incarnates the profound recognition that vulnerability, not power, engenders love. It is embodiment—most particularly, the limitations that come with fleshly existence—that connects us to each other.

Richard Rohr, one of my teachers, cautions those drawn to spirituality not to succumb to the grievous dualism that has been created between the spiritual and material worlds. They are one and the same, he says. To be truly spiritual is not to evade or ignore the body but to inhabit this life completely.

Incarnation is becoming flesh, becoming a thing rocked by ecstasy and pain, subject to decay and limitation—and capable of love.

+++ +++ +++

One effect of our meander through the medical world has been a deeper sense of humility. There's just no way around it. The health-care system is designed to strip us of our (erroneous but oh-so-comforting) claims to independence and self-reliance. When we are taken into the system, we become suffering bodies like all the other suffering bodies, often without the grace of privacy or empathy. Losing my protective coloration of competence forces me into greater reliance on the Holy.

Another effect of this cardiological journey has been deeper reflection on the aging process. It's become clear that our relationship to the world of medicine can no longer be the simple "Do this and you'll be fine" of younger years. It's become "Do this, and it will help for a while; then do that; then maybe you can do something else if none of this works." And someday, it will all stop working.

When the end is clearer and nearer, daily reality becomes either a struggle against the inevitable or a deep commitment to live out each day of holy incarnation for the sheer joy of being alive and for the opportunity to be part of the meat of the earth. Oh, my dear brothers and sisters in the flesh; oh, all matter and spirit joined in joyous breath: For this good and limited life, let us cry out thanksgiving.

{ 12 }

Life, Death, and a Sparrow

One evening last April, I deliberately killed a bird. I held a tiny, white-crowned sparrow—no more than a ball of feathers shielding a pounding heart—in my bare hands. Then I broke its neck.

Because I have never intentionally ended an avian life before (we will ignore the chickens and turkeys who have been slaughtered by others on my behalf), I didn't know how to kill it. My attempt to put this tiny being—convulsing with salmonella—out of its misery was therefore marked by ineptitude. What started as a mercy killing became unintentional torture. I could barely stand myself when it was over. I hid the tiny carcass under a bed of leaves behind the woodshed and ran to the house to wash.

An hour after this event, I went to hear our local doctor tell the community about the new Medical Assistance in Dying Act.

+++ +++ +++

I've thought a lot about dying in my adult life. I don't think it's because I am particularly morbid. If I am, I'm in fashionable company these days, as it's a hot topic for the aging boomer generation. But death has been a conscious part of my life since my younger brother died of brain cancer more than forty years ago. In my young adult years, working with folks who had severe disabilities, I was forced to confront my own assumptions about what made someone human, what made life "life."

Then, when I came into ministry almost thirty years ago, I started sitting beside deathbeds. I learned about "no code," intractable pain, family distress, and the unpredictability of death. I learned about fidelity and compassion. Most importantly, I learned how uncomfortable it is to simply be present, to stand as a helpless witness, watching another's suffering.

Because of this long acquaintance, I have developed some opinions about dying. I have believed that the process has the capacity to catapult both the dying and the living into greater depth and love. I have believed that death can be the last and best growth point of life. I have also believed that everyone deserves pain relief—physical and spiritual—at the end of their life.

And I have believed that ending your life at your own hand, or the hand of another, can be a shortcut whereby you could miss the mystery and depth of what it is to be human.

+++ +++ +++

So, I found this new Act challenging. I've read the articles in the popular press, for sure. For some people, it appears to be a godsend and a beauty. But I've seen the other side too, where, for those left living, the decision was a wrenching act that couldn't be put to rest.

The presentation on medically assisted dying was clear, showing how the process worked and highlighting the safeguards. I was shocked, frankly, by the description of how quickly the actual process works—like ending the life of a dog. But during the discussion period, it became clear that my aversion was not mainstream thinking. For many of my friends and neighbors, the inevitable loss of control at the end of life is a horror, not a doorway into grace. While I saw the Act's restrictions as weak gates to protect against

undue pressure and family expedience, others saw them as unnecessary bureaucratic hurdles to personal control.

I can't say that I'm happy about this new law. But I also recognize that I have not had to watch a family member die in intractable pain. I have not had to live long years with a parent or
spouse whose body is present but whose mind is not.

Frankly, I don't know what the "right" answer is—if there is one.
What I do know is what it was like to kill that tiny bird. I know that
I was moved by compassion for its suffering. I also know that, in
spite of that compassion, my actions felt wrong.

+++ +++ +++

In my experience, there's almost always a self-centered nub to
my rage against suffering. Other people's suffering makes me uncomfortable. I want to be in charge, in control, to stop this thing
that makes me feel so ill at ease.

I can see now that I had an alternative to wringing the sparrow's
neck. I could have left it to die on its own, in its own time. If I felt
like intervention was required, I could have picked up that bird and
wrapped it in my heart's love, held it gently and breathed with it. I
know from experience that this kind of attention relieves human
suffering. I don't think I'm wrong to assume that it would ease a
tiny bird's passing.

I could have worked past my own disgust and fear. These are the
same things that constrict my being when I'm with a dying human.
But my discomfort was compounded by guilt—Did that bird get sick
from the seed I put out?—and some kind of atavistic fear: Is it going
to spread salmonella to my dog, who's way too interested in this
bird?

I wrote earlier that I killed the bird with my bare hands, but that
was a lie. I donned gardening gloves. I picked up that sparrow with
dirty, rubberized fingers because I was afraid of germs, because I

didn't have the patience to let it die on its own time. The song sparrow's suffering made me uncomfortable.

And when it was finally dead after my multiple attempts to snap its neck, I washed and washed like Lady Macbeth.

+++ +++ +++

I was remembering that April evening recently after visiting a friend who has a very painful—and terminal—form of cancer. During our time together, this friend asked me to be with him at the end of his life. Although our spiritual paths differ greatly, we recognize each other's hearts. Later in the same rambling conversation, he also expressed curiosity about medically assisted dying.

I could surely understand why. But the combination of the two—medically assisted dying, my presence—had me in an internal dither. What would I do if he decided to end his life? Could I still be there with him?

I was talking the situation over with George—well, truthfully, I was moaning about it to him. George reminded me that my role would not be to assist in the death, but to hold my friend and everyone involved in love. He pointed out that I can choose to hold any situation in love, even—maybe especially—when I am uncomfortable with the situation.

That's when I realized that refusing to be there would be, for me, the equivalent of donning rubber gardening gloves. Refusing to participate would keep me from getting my hands dirty. I wouldn't have to encounter the mystery and confusion, the ambiguity, the real human drama involved in that final letting go. I wouldn't have to take seriously the amount of pain that my friend has lived with—and doesn't want anymore.

I'd have to let go of control myself.

But saying yes to being there without considering the impact on me would be an abdication of my responsibility to myself.

+++ +++ +++

My friend died without medical assistance. And I still don't have any one-size-fits-all answer about "assisted death." Physicians I know tell me that if someone just stops eating, they will die within a few days to a few weeks. They also tell me that a very high percentage of patients can get satisfactory pain relief at the end of life if they have adequate palliative care. But since palliative care is expensive, I worry that the unstated leverage in this discussion will be cost/benefit questions rather than ethics. I worry about the slippery slope "assisted dying" introduces into our life together.

If my friend who was dying had asked me what I thought (he didn't), I would have shared what I've learned about the paradoxical beauty of the end of life. I would have helped him advocate for adequate pain control. I certainly would have suggested that he stop eating, if he was sure he wanted to die. But I'm pretty sure that I wouldn't have told him to just suck it up. My big-picture thoughts—the ultimate goal of the dying process, the needed revisions to the law, alternative mechanisms, ethical dilemmas—are worthless to a person ground down by excruciating pain. (And, as Helen Luke would say, a short pause here to consider the etymology of the word "excruciating.") But I'm just as sure that I need to be clear, for myself, what my own boundaries are.

So, I am left with a paradox, an impossible situation, a koan, a place where things cannot be reconciled, a place where there is no rule to follow that will keep me safe. There's only the willingness to live in the discomfort that love foists on us.

{ 13 }

The Alleluia Egg

One recent morning, as I walked Rose down the hill for her post-prandial stroll, it started snowing: small, round lumps of snow, somewhere short of hail but without the definition of flakes, drifting down from the sky. They were suitable accompaniment to the cold wind that had been whipping the lake to whitecaps the last two days.

This walk took place on Easter, and the snow reminded me of waking to an Easter blizzard years ago, when I was still young enough to be excited by the Easter egg hunt, wondering how we'd ever do it with all the snow on the ground.

For the DesCamps, the hunt was usually confined to family—I guess my mother figured that eight children were enough to handle. And since we lived in Michigan for a good deal of the time that I was a child, those egg searches often took place inside the house, since outside could be mud, rain, or—as in this case—snow.

I don't remember much about the particular day. I don't know if the blizzard kept us home from church, although I suspect not. I don't even remember who found the Alleluia egg, which entitled you to an extra chocolate treat in addition to your Easter basket. What I do remember is that some of the eggs were hidden in the back hall.

+++ +++ +++

The back hall was a separate area on the second floor of our big old house. In it were storage closets, a narrow, enclosed staircase to the main floor, and two tiny rooms used in years past for housing the maids. There were no radiators, so it was bitter cold in the winter. Except for getting something out of storage, no one braved the back hall from November to April. But, for some reason, my mother decided it would be a good place to conceal several eggs. So she did, and we found them. That is, we found almost all of them. The last one was discovered months later when, as in Hamlet, the summer occupant of one of the rooms "nosed" it.

That secret hiding place, so clandestine that even my mother couldn't remember it, turned out to be a problem. So too is it with the hiding places of my heart, I think—having nosed out a hidden, malodorous part of my personality just this week.

+++ +++ +++

The setting is the board of a nonprofit organization, which I chair. (Have you ever noticed how often negative character traits rear their heads precisely at the place where we are trying to do good?) The offender is a member of the board who has been blaming, bossing, and bowling over others for months. The trigger was yet another email, sent after a difficult but successful meeting—an email that threatened to undo much of our hard work. I finally realized that it wasn't enough to simply model good behavior. It wasn't enough to just say, "Please watch your tone of voice." I needed to get more direct.

The way I discovered this need was that I woke up pissed off, not just once, but three mornings in a row. I fumed, I fussed, and I lined up my arguments. I couldn't stop imagining scenarios: gaveling the miscreant to order, removing her from the board, saying something—anything—that would make her recognize the impact of her behavior and beg forgiveness. I prayed for this sinner, best as I could, and I asked for a private meeting.

Thanks be, my email asking for a meeting went astray.

Thanks be, I have a perceptive spouse.

On Thursday, after listening to me whinge for most of another day, George asked me, "Who does she remind you of?" I threw off a couple of names—old nemeses, all of them—but wasn't sure. But the next morning—as I prepared for meditation—I nosed out that long-hidden Easter egg.

She reminded me of myself.

Forceful? Check. Intelligent? Check. Passionate about her position? Check. Opinionated? Check. Unconscious about the impact of her behavior on others? Half a check, please! Able to talk so long and loud that a sane person would take off their long underwear, lined boots, insulated pants, fur coat, mittens, and toque in minus-forty-degree weather just to shut her up? Actually, I'm not that persuasive.

I was transported back years, to my earlier career as a lobbyist and the way I was willing to run over anyone who got in the way of what I considered right. I was transported back a few days to the disdain I'd expressed for a theological perspective I deemed half-baked. I was transported back a month to my ruthless critique of a sermon and the minister who delivered it. I saw, in that sneaky way that self-awareness opens our eyes, that the stuff I hate about this member of "my" board is what I hate about myself.

All my justifications smelled just about like that reeking Easter egg.

+++ +++ +++

This isn't the end of the story, of course. I really do have to sit down with this person and talk about finding a different way for us all to interact. But I think I'll be doing it differently than I'd planned a few days ago.

In addition to all this reflection on the difficult board situation, I had the great grace—on that same day that I got gobsmacked by my own intemperance—to run across this quotation from Laurence Freeman, OSB. Freeman is the director of the World Community for Christian Meditation, and he writes this to help people who are struggling in their practice with turbulence, anger, a hard heart, or indifference—all the myriad distractions that make us want to judge ourselves. He notes, "At the place where we accept our imperfection—and only there—grace comes to our aid. It is as natural as a dog running to its master and indeed, in this sense only, God is at our beck and call. God cannot resist humility."[1]

So, this stinking mess of unconscious projection that I discovered is not the last word. I'm not supposed to drown in shame. I'm just supposed to witness. I'm just supposed to accept that sometimes I am exactly the same kind of jerk as the jerk with whom I'm angry. This makes me irresistible to the Big Holy.

Alleluia indeed.

+++ +++ +++

[1]Laurence Freeman, "A Letter from Laurence Freeman OSB," in *Christian Meditation Newsletter* 33:4 (Winter 2009–2010), 4.

{ 14 }

I Piss on This

Our elderly dog Rose normally gets two walks a day. While I am the usual suspect for the longer afternoon adventure, George is the customary morning attendant. When he's traveling for work, however, the sunup stroll falls to me.

I don't mind this early morning walk at all, especially if I'm not on a tight schedule. I love to watch as the first light hits the mountains across the lake and gradually flows down to the level of our yard. Those early, pellucid rays make everything look rested, lovely.

Yesterday morning, George was gone. So I gathered the leash and the dog and headed out. If Rose's hips hold out, the usual route is down the front walk, up the driveway, and then down the road to the hairpin turn and back.

As I walked through the meadow that is our front yard, I was overwhelmed by beauty. The tallest grasses were glowing and waving, the crimson bee balm polka-dotting the golden aureoles. The shorter grasses had purple-gray plumes, and the drying lavender blossoms added fragrance and visual undertones. The final touch was contributed by the almost imperceptible coolness in the air that marks the end of summer. It was a flood of color, scent, and temperature so complete that I thought I might drown in it.

I paused on the path, and then turned again on the driveway, seeing the front yard as someone else would see it. I resolved to take pictures so I could show it to Oregon friends. *We did this*, I thought to myself. *George and I spent the time and the money and the energy to make this beautiful place, to make this place beautiful.* Feeling quite pleased with myself, I headed up the drive, Rose at my side.

+++ +++ +++

At the top of the hill, where we normally take a right downhill toward the hairpin, Rose pulled left—a frequent phenomenon when walking this old dog. Since I was in no hurry, I let her lead me up the road for a bit. She was clearly on the scent of something good.

After a few minutes of nosing around, Rose squatted and lifted her leg. I looked at the spot she'd marked with some curiosity. Sometimes, she pees on a pile of coyote or bear scat. Sometimes, it's a dead thing. Whatever the object, this ritual seems to be her way to inform the other dogs on the hill that a particular nasty bit of muck belongs to her. *I piss on this*, she proclaims. *I made this big mess. I killed this animal. Do not screw around with me.*

Yesterday, Rose's target was the flattened remains of a large garter snake, looking more like a worn-out bicycle tire than anything that ever moved of its own volition. As she turned and trotted away, I laughed and followed along.

When we reached the bend in the dirt road, I looked up to see a sea of wild golden grasses on the verge. Dotted among them were spent clover blooms—deep brown contrast to the shining glory—and Michaelmas daisies blooming in soft lavender, their bright gold centers echoing the grasses waving around them.

I stopped dead in my tracks. This was a piece of wasteland next to the road, not a contrived garden. How could it be as beautiful as our front yard that has cost so much of our money and our energy? I looked again. It was not as beautiful as our garden. It was more beautiful. The grasses were interwoven in an elegant way that I can only pray happens as our meadow matures. I thought to myself, *Thank you.* I thought to myself, *No one did this. This is the world be-ing its lovely self. This is what the Holy loves into being.*

At that moment, I saw my earlier claims about the front yard for the silliness they were. *We did this,* I had intoned to myself. But we hadn't. Yes, we gave ourselves to the project. We envisioned it and funded it and hired folks to help dig and plant. We watered and weeded and fertilized and pruned. But the real work of it—the fact that the plants grew and that they stood next to each other in such harmony—had little to do with us. The reality is that growing-ness is a gift. If we're lucky, we can help it along. But whatever makes a plant respond to water, light, and soil with vigor, color, and scent, whatever makes a plant soften toward its surroundings and harmo-nize—well, that's way out of our control.

I realized that my pissing claims were not all that different from Rose's.

+++ +++ +++

The metaphor stayed with me through the day, and I started see-ing how the desire to claim things as my own permeates my life. It's a natural human instinct, this longing to take credit for what I think I have accomplished. *I did this,* the self trumpets. *I made this happen.* I urinate on my figurative kill to let myself and others know that I am important, that I am of worth. The more uncertain I feel about my value, the more I spray.

A few incidents from the past came flooding back. One involved a phone call about a year after I moved here. Feeling untethered from my professional identity, I was overjoyed to get an invitation to help after the sudden death of a village member. "Of course I'm available to do whatever is needed," I said, imagining that someone had finally noticed my great skills in pastoral counseling, my years of experience supporting grieving families. Then the person on the other end of the line told me that the family was looking for some-

one to care for the dog when they drove into town to the cremato-
rium. My initial reactions were fury—*Can't they see what I have to offer?*—and crushing embarrassment.

I said yes. But what I wanted, truthfully, was less about being of
use and more about cocking my leg. I longed to claim something as
my own, to say, "I do this. I am important. People need me."

+++ +++ +++

Not all my memories of micturition are metaphorical. When
George and I initially traveled to New Denver to look for land, we
were hoping for a place close to town with enough privacy and
room for a retreat center. We'd looked at bare acreage, homes in the
woods, even a lakefront property or two. Both of us felt drawn by
this piece of property above Carpenter Creek, on the mountainside
overlooking the village. On that October afternoon, when the real
estate agent had gone home, we returned to the land.

It had been a number of hours since lunch and the several cups of
coffee required to warm me on a damp, cold day. George decided to
walk the upper bench, while I wandered alone among the wild roses
on the lower bench. Necessity called, and I relieved my bladder. But
that leak in the bush was more than necessity. There was a very real
sense in which my peeing was a claim. *This is the place,* I said to myself. *This is our land,* I said to myself. And indeed, after a few months
of difficult negotiation, it did indeed become "ours."

+++ +++ +++

There's a problem with the need to urinate on things. Rose has
shown me this. When we're strolling through an area that other dogs
frequent, she works hard. She's required to stop and squat every few
feet, marking over other scents, for the entire journey. And every
time someone else comes by and lets loose on whatever she has pre-

viously claimed, she has to do it all over again. It takes a lot of energy for an old dog with bad hips. It also takes a lot of urine. Sometimes, she simply gives up.

A while back—when a necessary piece of construction wasn't getting done, when my writing was faltering—I was whining to a friend about how much work it took to "hang on to the land." This wasn't the first time I'd complained to her. But on this occasion, she gently pointed out that I'd misread my task. My work, she said, was to care for what God had entrusted into our safekeeping. Whether we made things balance financially wasn't the true measure. The real standard was whether we were loving the land and the work which we'd been given for however long it was ours to tend.

At that moment, I felt a reshaping of our purpose. Combined with the rain of years gone by, this new vision has, I think, effectively washed my mark off the land. I can now say, "You are mine to care for. You are my joy, my burden, my gift, for however long I can serve you. Thank you for letting me live here."

+++ +++ +++

Now, I don't think that all these particular pissings were wrong. My squat on the lower bench bound me to this place and this work, and that was good. The desire to be of service in an area where I feel competence is likewise a good thing. My pleasure in the beauty of the front yard is certainly a human joy and therefore another good.

But in the end, my best guide is probably not my inner dog, lifting her leg on all that she claims. It is my inner heart, which tends—and releases— everything in joy.

{ 15 }

Taller than a Dog

As I took Dolly the dog out for our early morning walk, I spotted her best friend down the street. Dolly, whose head rises a little over eighteen inches off the ground, could see only the driveway rising in front of her. I, being five feet six, could see over the rise of the drive and down the roadway two blocks to the corner, where Kaia was sitting.

At that moment, I became a visionary and a prophet. Because of my wide-angle view, I could see what was going to happen before it happened. I knew that Dolly and Kaia were destined to meet on the road sometime in the next thirty seconds, joyously whining and wagging and sniffing each other's bottoms. It was as if the future had been laid out on a spatial plane.[1]

When spiritual teachers talk about consciousness, they're not talking about the kind of barely conscious existence that marks so much of our lives—like when I find myself grabbed by the news and not able to notice that my jaw is painfully clenched. Consciousness, in spiritual terms, is a quality of attention. It is non-reactive: Attention is not *taken by* something, but rather *given to* something. Paying attention becomes a matter of choice rather than something that happens to me. This form of attention is work. What it means right now is that I have to choose to concentrate on writing instead of checking my email or getting up for a cup of tea or any other of the millions of distractions the world offers.

Those millions of distractions can seem awfully important. I will confess that I spent much of yesterday glued to a news feed about a particularly ugly piece of bad behavior in our neighboring nation. As the mess of the world continues unabated—which it always does—I expect that there will be other days when I find my attention well and thoroughly grabbed—when I descend into mechanical being rather than a focused point of attention.

But most days, I fight this unconscious behavior because it puts me down at doggy-eye level.

+++ +++ +++

When I'm in the world of consciousness-grabbing stuff, I can't see any further than the road that rises in front of me. It becomes impossible to imagine anything other than what's right ahead. There's no future different from the present that I see down here at ground level.

But when we rise up taller than a dog, so to speak—when we free ourselves from being grabbed, when we calm down and look out over the landscape—life takes on a different quality. If our standpoint is geological time, we are just one of the millions of species that come and go. From the historical view, civilizations rise and fall. From a cosmic perspective, we see the endless creativity of the universe. And from the vantage point of the shimmering depths of Oneness, we simply dwell in the love that connects everything, regardless.

But...there's something more than just a bigger perspective at work when we're taller than a dog. This new vantage point also allows us to think about causality in a different way.

In the normal, dog's-eye-view world, life progresses along in a linear fashion. "A" happens, which causes "B," which causes "C." Causality is linear. It is simply the way things are.

But notice, please, when you're up above and can see more broadly—like I was on that winter morning last week—how the center becomes causal. From the taller-than-a-dog perspective, it is the inevitable tail-wagging meeting which drew each dog from her own warm home to run down a cold, dark street. The center of the story exerted an influence which moved the players. This was no linear accident, but a concentric design. The butt-sniffing dénouement causes the beginning.

When we see from this viewpoint, it makes a different kind of sense of the incredibly messy world in which we are living. From the taller-than-a-dog perspective, the transformation of the world—of which so many of us dream—is exerting a strong magnetic influence. There is a sense of being drawn forward rather than pushed from behind. Our longing for a more just world pulls us toward deeper commitment. Even as the world goes up in flames and people behave badly, we are tugged more deeply into love of these people, this biosphere. As we struggle toward some collective magnitude of consciousness—a new level of evolution—it seems like that new consciousness is reaching back to help us.

This perspective helps me make sense of the profound disturbances we're experiencing right now. Resistance to change always becomes stronger as change becomes more inevitable. We have to go through a kind of hell to be willing to chance the next transformation. That's certainly been true for me, individually, and I am inclined to think that the collective "we" functions in much the same way. It's terrifying, giving up the way we understand the world. Few of us do it graciously. Yet we are inexorably tugged along.

So, it's a good time to remind ourselves where we want to stand and what we see from that graced lookout. The view does not exempt us from our humanity, from suffering the sorrows of these days and the hard work required to bring things right. But knowing that we are being drawn forward allows us to find the flow, to surf the currents pulling us toward that central causality. From this perspective, we can quit worrying about where things are going and simply play our part as lovers of the whole grand and awful mess of things.

+++ +++ +++

[1]I was introduced to this perspective of imaginal causality by Cynthia Bourgeault in her book *Mystical Hope: Trusting in the Mercy of God* (Cloister Books, 2001).

{ 16 }

Matchless

Years ago, I went to a weeklong retreat on healing prayer. (If the idea of healing prayer creeps you out because you think of TV faith healers, I agree. I only went to this after a long and large shift in my own understanding of the Holy Infinite, and prayer, and what really constitutes healing.)

I didn't really know what to expect, but the work was straightforward enough that I didn't feel the need to run away. There were, for sure, some totally weird moments, like when—in an attempt to help us focus our attention—we were each given a book match. You know the kind: It comes inside a little paper cover with an advertisement for some tavern and a tiny striking pad. When you open the packet, there are maybe twenty matches, each made of rough, gray-brown paper with a red chemical head. We were each given one of those matches.

Part of me got quite excited—Were we finally going to do something weird? Were we going to be taught to set the match on fire with our minds? But the first thing the teacher said was, "We are not going to be setting these matches on fire with our minds." (Bitter disappointment and internal embarrassment.) Then he said, "I am setting the timer for ten minutes. For the next ten minutes, I would like you to attend to your match. You can feel it, sniff it, taste it, look at it. What you cannot do is make up a story about it. Don't look for the face of Jesus. Don't trace the history of the wood and chemicals that composed it. Don't think about its usefulness in the world. Simply look at the match. Whenever you find yourself making a story, come back to simply observing."

Holy shit, I thought. *This is going to be profoundly boring.*

It wasn't.

+++ +++ +++

Because we did the match exercise three or four times each day during that week, I learned to pay attention to that book match. Here's what I perceived: layers of gray-brown paper; their thickness and thinness; the way the paper furred out on the edges as the fibers came apart; the way that you could sometimes see the wood cells intact in the paper; the way the layers came apart at the bottom, where the match was torn from the match book; the softness of the edges; the straight little bits of wood fiber in the paper; the way that the bright red head reflected light in certain places, as well as the colors of that light—blue, gold, green; how the lower part of the head curved down the stem of the match; how the top of the head differed in shape from one side to the other; the bulge at the top; the pointed corner; the air bubbles trapped in the red chemical head, and how they lined up with each other; and on, and on, and on.

When I state that I attended to my book match, I don't mean that I felt slobbery over it or made it into something other than it was. I saw that match's integrity, its composition, its reality. I valued it for itself—no more, no less, and I found myself perfectly satisfied to do that exercise over and over.

As far as I can tell, attention is the deepest love I can offer.

+++ +++ +++

Fast forward ten years or so. It's an early morning, and I am hauling rocks. Whether pushing a full wheelbarrow through bracken fern along the lower bench or creeping down the steep road in the heavily laden four-wheel drive, that summer I was engaged in moving the stuff of our landscape into a new pattern. I was constructing a labyrinth.

I learned about attention in a new way through these weeks of rock work. I learned to attend to the size and shape of stones, their heft, their center of gravity, their color, and their width and height. Most of all, I learned to notice how a given rock wants to stand on the land and what kind of land it seeks to stand on.

Some of this learning came quickly. I didn't think, when we were clearing the land, laying out the landscape fabric, and drawing the eleven-circuit, forty-four-foot-wide pattern, about how the rocks were going to be placed. I just assumed that we would put them on the ground and that would be that. But it was hard to ignore that the land was not flat, even after the front-end-loader guy cleared the space. It was lumpen, with cobbles and roots and hummocks. My very own knees and hands told me all about it as I crawled around on the landscape cloth, drawing the design. I realized that I had been dealing with an idealized image of the ground—groomed, level, featureless. Real ground was very different from my fantasies.

+++ +++ +++

In the beginning, I'd tote a boulder over to that huge empty space and position it flat side down. Then, it would fall over because the ground was uneven. Or I'd put a stone in place, and it would roll to one side and block the path because I hadn't noticed the slope of the surface underneath it. Or I'd walk over with the perfect rock and suddenly see that there was a huge tree root under the landscape cloth.

I panicked for a while. The task felt impossible—and impossibly more complex than I had planned. But over time, I learned to see the ground more clearly. I saw the rocks more clearly too. Just as the ground was nothing like flat, the rocks were nothing like uniform.

+++ +++ +++

I began to pick up rocks and heft them in my hands, just getting a sense of them. I didn't do anything analytical, like calculate their weight or width or planes. I'd just start walking, and they would tell me where to go—not in words, of course. But I began to get an internal sense that wasn't logical and wasn't verbal. I'd just start walking, paying attention to when I felt moved to stop, or turn, or shift things around.

Some of the rocks asked to be placed next to each other in order to mutually steady themselves. Some of them informed me that while they were too wide for the regular path, they were well suited to the places where paths met or to the outer edges. Some asked to join the design even though they were too small or misshapen to stand alone, finding their homes in nooks and crannies or on top of others. Some showed me that their points were especially suited to demarcation of the inner rosette. But most of them asked me only to notice carefully whether the slope of the ground in a particular place—a slope which had been previously imperceptible to me—helped them to stay upright or caused them to list.

+++ +++ +++

Laurence Freeman, OSB, the Director of the World Community for Christian Meditation, writes, "Attention...is the true heart of prayer, as well as the secret of every human relationship."[1] Or as Jesus says in Matthew 6:2, "Where your treasure is, there your heart will be also."

+++ +++ +++

The same summer that I built the labyrinth, a friend slid into her own private hell. An old, self-destructive behavior came back, and with it flashbacks to a horrendous childhood. One Friday night, it all came crashing down on her. The thing she needed most was presence: someone to hear what was happening, to help her remember what she knew about being whole, to sit with her so she wasn't alone in her agony. She chose me.

Of course, it wasn't a convenient time. We had a houseful of people, and I had a writing deadline to meet. But the bigger issue was that I had no clue how to respond to all the pain I was hearing. All I knew was that I had to be as intently present as I had ever been in my life. So, I listened with one ear tuned to her and the other ear tuned to the Holy, in hopes of guidance.

When the crisis had passed, she acknowledged just how much she appreciated the support and how difficult the timing had been for me. My response, which surprised me, was not to deny the strain. Instead, what came out of my mouth was, "I guess that's how we know we love each other."

+++ +++ +++

What I meant, I think, is that I knew she must trust and love me to tell me such painful truths about herself. I also meant that the kind of attention I gave to her was a form of love, expressed through my willingness to listen long and deep and to simultaneously attend to the whisper of the Holy. Love was essential because I felt so inadequate to the task, and yet I didn't run away.

The long hours with the matches and the long hours on the labyrinth had prepared me to be silent and curious about things I didn't understand. Who knew that book matches, varied rocks, and uneven ground would teach me how to love?

+++ +++ +++

[1]Laurence Freeman, "A Letter from Laurence Freeman OSB," *Christian Meditation Newsletter* 30, no. 1 (March 2006), 4.

PART III: SO I FOLD THEM IN PRAYER

{ 17 }

Power Surges and Epiphanies

One of the realities of rural living is that our electrical power is, shall we say, a little iffy. As I understand it, when you live in an urban area, your electricity usually comes from multiple sources and gets mixed in the grid before it reaches your house. There are redundant circuits as well as redundant protections. When one of those electrical sources or circuits has a power surge or loss, you may experience a blip in your lights, but normally the system can right itself without much pain and suffering in your household.

But here in the sticks, our power comes from a single source, strung on poles through miles of forested mountains. In these forests are many big trees, and fat wet snow falls on those big trees, subsequently causing some of those big trees to fall on those lines. Since the poles hold not only the lines carrying the huge wads of power into the substation, but also the smaller lines out of the substation that carry electricity to our rural homes, sometimes—like this last week—trees fall, lines cross, and transformers blow up. Then a surge of power comes ripping down the wires, exploding into a big blue light show visible all over town, blowing out the substation, which takes with it computers, electrical panels, stoves, and—in this household—the controls and compressor for the geothermal heat.

In a stunning series of multiple power outages, we lost not only our geothermal heat, our electric boiler backup, and the smoke alarms, but also the surge protector at the pole and the two surge protectors built into the electrical panels. Which, I suppose, means that those surge protectors worked—at least in part. After all, we didn't lose the fridge or freezer or our computers.

Our friend Brian, an electrician, explained it to me the next morning as we stood in the frigid back hallway, staring at the small black box with a hole blown in its side. The surge protector is supposed to take all that extra energy and ground it into a bed of sand, where it dissipates. All that big energy gets distributed out into something that can handle it. That's the key—it has to be able to handle it.

+++ +++ +++

Now for epiphany, which fits better here than you might think. I suppose that this word has been on my mind because the Christian feast of Epiphany—when the wise men show up in Bethlehem to see the baby—took place recently. From that day until the start of Lent is referred to as the Epiphany season.

One definition of epiphany is a precipitous, intuitive leap of understanding; an all-of-a-sudden knowing; a blare of trumpets and flash of insight in the middle of mundane life. An epiphany can also designate the appearance of a god; hence, the recent celebration. In the Western church, this marks the joyous arrival of the Magi. In the Eastern church, the feast was initially associated with the birth of Christ. The season of Epiphany includes the wise men now, but also Jesus's baptism and transfiguration—other times when the Ultimate Infinite was recognized in Jesus.

+++ +++ +++

In my experience, that first kind of epiphany—the sudden, intuitive jolt—feels a lot like a power surge. I'm basically a shortcut girl, so I like this. But it's not always pleasant, to say the least. I've had a few of those blasts in my past: in a therapist's office years ago, when

a few words changed my self-definition from normal drinker to alcoholic; in seminary, having a comfortable cup of coffee with my
best friend George, when I realized that I was madly in love with
him; once, over a lunch discussion, when I morphed from an ordi-
nary struggling minister into someone who was leaving her church.

These epiphanies aren't necessarily about the appearance of a
god (George might want to argue with that one!) but more about
the appearance of a hidden truth, the way that all the loose ends
come together suddenly and definitively. I live my life not knowing
what I don't know, and then suddenly, BANG! I know. Once I know,
once some truth has come clear, there's no going back. Then I'm left
to figure out what the hell to do with this new knowledge.

Which brings me back to surge protectors. What protects us from
completely frying when a big charge like this comes down the wire?

If we are lucky, the gradual living of life has given us sufficient
structure—sturdy character—that can act as a shock absorber in
shocking times. This is not the same as denial. This is the hard work
of repeatedly absorbing and integrating suffering and discourage-
ment. This is learning to stand steady during the times when we
want to throw up our hands and walk away. With character, we
learn how to deal with the (sometimes-horror of a) new situation
and grow rather than burrow into the ground of deadening fear.

But sometimes, even with sturdy character, we get blown out to a
place we don't know how to handle. We find ourselves walking in
the dark wood, not knowing what to do next, not understanding
how we can possibly go on. Which brings me to another kind of
surge protector: community.

+++ +++ +++

When I figured out I was a drunk, I knew that I needed to stop
drinking but had no idea how. I had the great good luck that there
existed a group of people who had sorted sobriety out and who gave

freely of their time to assist me. Likewise, when I decided to quit being a pastor, I called on friends and colleagues who had been through similar transitions.

This works at the physical level too. This past week, when we were shivering in the sub-zero cold, our friends and neighbors volunteered wood and warm rooms to stay in. When the electricity went back on, they offered plug-in heaters to keep the pipes from freezing. Community saved us, again.

There is also, I think, a third kind of surge protector—the voice of our unconscious, our soul. Listening to this voice brings us into a different relationship with the blast of power that's headed our way. This may be most obvious if we use the second definition of epiphany—the appearance of a god. Specifically, the appearance of the Christ in the traditional story of the Wise Men.

I can see how the two definitions of epiphany are related, why recognizing a god is considered a sudden and intuitive thing. Maybe it usually is. But the occurrence that we commemorate twelve days after Christmas was anything but precipitate. While the appearance of the Magi must have felt all-of-a-sudden to Mary and Joseph (and probably Herod too), for the wise men there was no quick realization, no speedy denouement, nothing fast. There was just a long, long slog down a long, long road, hoping beyond hope that you weren't making the trip in vain and not sure where you'd end up or what you'd find. From the example of the travelers from the East, it would appear that sometimes we do know what we don't know, or at least we anticipate what we don't know: We hope for it, plan for it, and structure our life as if it were true.

+++ +++ +++

I've recently returned to John Tarrant's book *The Light Inside the Dark*. Tarrant, a Jungian psychotherapist and Zen Buddhist, is a profound and tender observer of the human condition. What I stumbled over a few days ago speaks to the kind of epiphany that the Magi experienced—the appearance of the Divine after a tedious, faithful slog:

> When we want to do something, we turn our hearts toward it and eventually a path opens. Much of the preparation for the inward work lies in developing the intention to do it, [in] making it more important than going to a movie or being admired by our friends. It is not enough to long for freedom—we must have a platform in daily life, a basis for the change. Change itself is sudden, like harvest. It is preparing the ground that takes time.[1]

It seems that epiphany—either that sudden, intuitive understanding or the appearance of a god—can affect us in two ways. It can spring on us like a power surge, blowing our circuits, or it can invite us to turn toward it in expectation and mystery. In the first way, the cost comes after the event as we struggle to understand and rearrange our lives to accommodate this new way of being. In the second way, we pay the big cost up-front. It's less dramatic and leaves us open to self-doubt and possibly derision during that long waiting time. But that's faith: the preparation of the ground of ourselves to receive the unfathomable Divine.

When I was a kid and went to Mass every day, we would recite this phrase: *We wait in joyful hope for the coming of our savior, Jesus Christ.* That line, which encapsulates the long path of faith, still raises a thrill in me. Here's what I am longing for today: a surge protector that really works, the slow epiphany, and the willingness to walk the long, tenebrous road with joy and inner certainty.

+++ +++ +++

[1]John Tarrant, *The Light Inside the Dark: Zen, Soul, and the Spiritual Life* (Harper, 1998), 193.

{ 18 }

On the Spectrum

"Are we all going through a dark night of the soul?" he asked. "That's what one of my teachers said last week."

I have pondered that question for a month and have decided that I disagree. I do believe that we are all suffering, whether we are conscious of this fact or not. But we are not all going through a spiritual dark night—in fact, far from it. Over time, I've come to believe that there are four main ways that we are dealing with these post-pandemic, deeply divisive times: delusion, denial, depression, and spiritual dark night. We're probably all invited into the dark night, but I'm not sure that we're all accepting the invitation. As a matter of fact, I'm quite sure that I am regularly turning it down and taking a detour into something more comfortable. So I think that it might be helpful to check in with ourselves, using these categories, as we live into these difficult times.

Delusion

One response to this time is sinking deeply into delusion. Whether fed by the right or the left, many of us have come to believe that the "other" people are wicked, duped, or part of a vast conspiracy of corruption and domination. We are aided and abetted in our delusions by the way that social media operates (algorithms that feed us more of the same kind of thing we just looked at), by our evolutionary physiology (which predisposes us to expect the worst), and by our psychological need for control (which keeps us scanning the worst of the worst so that we are "prepared" for what is coming).

Whether perpetrated by the self (in a vain attempt to control the oh-so-unpredictable future) or by others (and yes, I do admit that some people are using this time to grab power), delusion renders us unable to work together. Delusion sets tests (*Do you believe what I believe?*), and if the other doesn't pass the test, they are automatically relegated to the realm of less-than-human. This is the precursor for violence and injustice.

When I find myself having thoughts about other groups of people—like feeling certain that everyone on the "other side" is corrupt—I realize that I'm heading into delusion. I am simplifying life to make myself feel safe, seeing through a way-too-small lens, doing exactly what I have accused the disparaged "other" of doing.

Denial

My personal favorite among these responses is denial. Denial tells me that if I just put my head down and eat a little more, watch another movie, or drink a little more, I won't have to feel.

Denial differs from delusion in that denial doesn't admit that there's a problem. "This is how I prefer to live my life anyway" or "I don't really think things are that bad" are the remarks that roll off my lips when I'm in denial. In denial, I'm not viewing anyone else as the enemy. In fact, I'm not seeing anyone else at all. Two million people dead? Kids in my community without food? Rising numbers of white supremacists? Hey, I've got chocolate and a book.

I want to freely admit that I engage in denial regularly—every day, for that matter. I don't know how I would survive if I didn't let my overburdened psychic and emotional systems rest. We all need to shut the door on the suffering and confusion for a while. The amount of information and change that we are all facing is enormous and exhausting.

But when we find ourselves *nailing* the door after we've shut it or engaging in really lovely things like meditation or the taste of a good chocolate bar compulsively—as a way to stuff those feelings into a dark, secure corner—that's denial.

Where delusion blames, denial is blind. Other beings aren't evil. Instead, they're wallpaper which we feel free to ignore.

Depression

Sometimes, people confuse depression and a spiritual dark night. In both these states, we feel the loss of pleasure. We are overwhelmed with a sense of our inadequacy. And both are deeply painful times. But there are two deformities of the psyche that belong only with depression: the absence of humor and the absence of compassion.

When I'm mired in a depression, I am incapable of humor. I sure as hell can't poke fun at myself. The only thing resembling laughter is sarcasm. I turn away from the comic side of life, dwelling in a bitterness that is infectious. One psychologist said that he could diagnose depression by how he felt after he'd been with someone who's depressed: depleted, deflated.

When I'm depressed, I am not only incapable of joy. I am also incapable of seeing anyone's pain but my own. If I do happen to observe someone else's pain, I usually translate it into something that's about me, like when I convince myself that I am so exquisitely and uniquely sensitive that I can't even bear to hear about others' suffering. My compassion is nonexistent. As with denial, other people constitute the wallpaper in the room, but this wallpaper is mirrored, forever reflecting me back at myself.

I want to recognize here that depression is a profoundly painful cycle, one that often requires medication to free us up to do the work we need to do. Unlike delusion and denial—where our suffering is masked from us by repetitive behaviors and opinions—in depression, we're keenly aware of our suffering.

Dark Night

I'm not going to distinguish between dark night of the senses and dark night of the spirit except to explain that in the first, we lose pleasure in outer things, while in the second, we lose pleasure in inner things. That constitutes a real difference in spiritual terms, but in day-to-day functioning, I think it's safe to say that dark nights *do* involve loss of meaning, loss of joy, and loss of certainty. Doubt and self-doubt are regular visitors, as is deep sorrow.

But if I'm experiencing a dark night, I will still be able to see the humorous side of life. I will be capable of laughter. I may feel deeply the sadness, confusion, and horror of these times—and I may not expect things to get much better. But I can laugh, and most often at myself. I take myself lightly.

Even more clearly, I will be capable of compassion. The dark night does not reduce our capacity to care for others. Rather, it increases that capacity. In fact, some days, caring for others may be the only thing that relieves the suffering of having lost my bearings.

Dark nights don't involve a diminution of self, but rather a shift in focus away from the ego and onto others. I may no longer have the consolation of feeling like I'm a good person or experiencing closeness to the "God" that I used to know so intimately. But daily life will be filled with the awareness of the preciousness of all life.

Where delusion makes the "other" an enemy, denial makes the "other" into wallpaper, and depression reduces the "other" to my mirror, the dark night heightens our connections to all living beings. In a dark night, I feel deeply the sorrow—as well as the joy—of the other. It may be dark in here, but it's full of love.

So I think it's worth keeping track of where I am on this spectrum during these parlous and uncertain times. Am I creating an alternative reality that must be defended? Am I lost in numbness? Am I focused entirely on my less-than-adequate self? Or am I feeling the pain and doubt and suffering of these times and compassionately extending the love that I don't necessarily feel but that I trust pours through me?

{ 19 }

Little White Socks

This was the scene about two weeks ago: It's early Sunday morning, George is in Grand Forks, and I am sitting in my usual place, cross-legged on the floor in meditation. My leg goes to sleep, a common occurrence. The thought crosses my mind that I need to switch positions. Then comes a second, appealing alternative—just settle more deeply into meditation and you won't notice the discomfort. I ignore the first thought because I have a hard time respecting my body. I choose the second because I like to prove how deeply spiritual I am. I choose it because deep down I still believe that gratuitous suffering is good for me.

I'm deep when the phone rings—George calling from Grand Forks. But my leg is asleep. First thought: Crawl to the phone. Second, appealing alternative: It might be interesting to walk on this. What a strange sensation, I think as I stand and fling my leg forward. Wow. I am totally without feeling from the hip down.

Two steps later, feeling is instantaneously restored as I fracture my foot.

Now, it's a bright, cold day with snow on the ground and sun on the glacier. But I'm not out walking Rose, I'm not cooking dinner, and I'm not even sitting at my desk. Instead, I am in front of the woodstove, feet on the stool, laptop on my lap. This is where I've been for twelve days, and where I'll be for several more weeks. And on my feet are little white socks.

I put these socks on after I rub my feet with anti-inflammatory oil. When I need to get around, one sock is replaced by a knee-length cast. These socks, which make my feet look unprotected and vulnerable, have a history. They are an inheritance from my mom. My mother wore these white cotton anklets when the varicose veins—a direct result of carrying so many babies—broke open on her ankles. Every few years, she'd have a flare-up, spend weeks or months with her feet up most of the day, shuffle around on crutches, and be unable to go walking. After my father's death, when she lived in an apartment all by herself, these episodes got much more difficult. She had help from friends and her kids, but mostly she managed on her own. When I was in town, I would come over and cook and care for her, but I confess that I often found myself nagging her to stay down more, wondering why she chafed so, wondering why she couldn't just accept that she was an old person and limited.

Right now, I feel like my mom. It's not just the white socks. I am—temporarily, I trust—unable to carry things. I find that it hurts to stand for long periods of time. I can't go rambling outside, and I can't even drive because it's my right foot where the overstretched tendon tore off a piece of bone.

Also like my mom, I've had some lovely help. Friends have walked Rose, brought groceries, straightened up my house, and fixed food. George cancelled a trip to Vancouver to keep the home fires burning (literally) and carry my teapot to the meditation area each morning.

And like my mom, I've gotten a lot of well-meaning advice. I wonder now how she could stand me telling her what to do, interpreting her life for her.

Forgive me for that, Mom.

+++ +++ +++

On Tuesday, George took me to the clinic for a short consult and then we swung by the library so I could snag a few recreational books. As I hobbled in, I passed an older man in a wheelchair. I found I could barely look at him. I was struck with horror at aging, at the prospect of permanently losing my veneer of competence. How do we come to grips with this? The mind boggles. No matter how well I plan, it's likely that I'll face that time when I am unable to care for myself physically. And if I'm like a lot of people I've known, being unable to care for myself physically may mean that my capacity to care for myself emotionally and spiritually will be precarious. Who am I if I can't produce? What good am I if my body won't do what I want it to do?

Yesterday, after I'd "done too much"—i.e., gotten ferried down-town for an hour to find Christmas presents for our granddaughter and then spent another two hours hopping up and down in choir practice—I found myself plummeted into the hell of infirmity. No matter how much I bucked myself up, I couldn't put strength into my arms, keep my left leg sturdy and painless, and stay safely up-right to do my usual tasks. "I am a useless old woman," spoke my mother in my voice. The whole list of synonyms spilled forth: incompetent, inept, ineffective, incapable, unemployable, inadequate, hopeless, no-account, bad, pathetic.

+++ +++ +++

I like to find the layers of meaning in my life. That's what it is to be religious. Like a student of the Kabbalah, like a monk practicing daily self-examination, I mine the events and feelings of my day to find hidden patterns, to see *why*. Sometimes, this is a useful way to consider my past behavior: If I'd listened to my body, I wouldn't have fractured my foot. But often, it's a way to learn how I should go forward, how to accept what feels unacceptable.

I resist, however, the notion that all that happens is for some purpose. This is not to say that I don't find God in my present frailty. I do. When I was lying on a massage table Sunday night and six women—three of whom I'd barely met—held me in healing prayer, I found God in their care. I found God in the generosity of the friend who ironed the tablecloth for Saturday night's dinner party, in the friend who made healing oil, in the friend who is picking me up for choir tonight. I find God in George's cooking, and dishwashing, and hauling of ice packs, and in his patience with my ineptitude and grief. I especially find God in the painful experience of asking for, and accepting, help.

But when I say that I don't think this is for some purpose, I mean that I don't believe God did this, or planned it, or necessarily wants things this way. (Well, maybe. I'm human, so I don't know, right?) But the way I understand the Holy these days, my God works in all situations for good but does not, by any stretch of the imagination, desire that all those situations occur.

If I'm going to slap on the bumper sticker that says Grace Happens, I want to stick Shit Happens right beside it. I think of the news of the past two weeks—the child of my heart who is living on the street, the grandbaby who died before she was born, the friend who has cancer, the other friend who was fired, the two whose parents died suddenly in the midst of vibrant older age. To me, none of this looks good. None of it, at least on the surface, reads like wholeness or joy or freedom. It looks more like shit. I can only call this "God's will" in that it is the reality of life on earth.

And yet, when suffering occurs, I must believe that grace is never far away. Some would say this is self-delusion, protecting myself from the misery of reality. Maybe. But since I know that changing my conceptual frame changes my perception of reality, and since the human brain is constructed so that bad things stick more than good things—they are more accessible in memory and more vivid than pleasant events—I practice seeing good, seeing joy, seeing grace. It's as much a spiritual discipline as cross-legged meditation. So, this morning, when I was done weeping and raging about my decrepitude and George said, "We have to find the joy," I tried.

+++ +++ +++

The other day, a Buddhist friend asked me how I prepare for Christmas. I told her that usually I would be thinking about how to tell the Christmas story in a way that tired adults could really hear it. "So how would you do that?" she pressed. I found myself speaking about the feelings of the last two weeks: about how it hurts to be powerless; about the way we humans spend our lives clutching for safety, grabbing food and money and status, while the Divine chose to come in weakness and poverty; about my heart's softening when I accept my limits; about the fact that when I give up trying to fix things, trying to make the world conform to my desires, I am able to dwell in the goodness of life; about the hidden holiness of vulnerability; and finally, and most importantly, about how love is the only power worth having.

From the perspective of the coming season, my fractured foot and its accompanying small tribulations—all that's represented by these little white socks—are the reminders I need of the essence of the good life. This good life is not based on what I'm able to own or accomplish, but on my willingness to let go of my expectations, to release my death grip on safety, mastery, and competence. It is God's will, if you please, for me to be vulnerable. It is not pleasing to me, this human impotence. But it appears to be necessary because it is in my poverty—my essential defenselessness against the realities of life—that I most need, and best receive, love.

{ 20 }

My Mother's Teeth

We had been piecing it together for months. My mother, after living for eight years on her own, needed help. We'd started by hiring someone to clean, then added someone to prepare her meals, then someone to help her get up and go to bed. Finally, painfully, it became clear that she needed to move from her eighth-floor independent apartment to the nursing floor—to the ground floor.

On the day in question, I was unpacking the few things that might make the tiny room feel like home. The past few days had been long, hot, and sad. The diminishment of her life, the loss that lay ahead, crouched like a presence in her room.

When the evening care aide came in to help her get ready for bed, I continued putting things away but listened closely, alert for error. The nursing staff was still getting to know her, and I wanted them to understand that my intelligent, thoughtful mother might be diminished physically, might be suffering some memory loss, but she was still here. She was still vital. I didn't want them talking down to her. The need to protect my vulnerable mama felt like a ferocious fire in my chest.

I could hear that something was wrong. I poked my head around the corner and realized that the young woman assisting my mom was pulling, hard, at her mouth. "What's going on?" I asked anxiously, angrily.

"Her dentures won't come out," said the girl. "They're stuck."

+++ +++ +++

Here's the thing about my mother. Her father (whom we all called Papa) was a dentist in a little town, and he put braces on her very crooked teeth when she was a youngster. Soon after, she contracted strep throat and almost died. Papa was so horrified that he wouldn't ever work on her teeth again. Since there was no other dentist around, my mom ended up with terrible, crooked teeth, full of cavities. All her life they had caused her misery and embarrassment.

After a long conversation with the aide and the charge nurse, we figured out that some other aide had used a dental adhesive in her mouth that morning. My mom had told them that she didn't use it. Her dentures didn't require it. But someone had decided that she didn't know what she was talking about. So now those dentures were locked tight on her bleeding gums.

I was so furious that I wanted to burn the place down. All my grief, all my loss, and all my fear was focused like an angry laser on that young care aide.

My mother's thin hand reached out and softly patted my arm. I could see her veins and bones through translucent skin. "TC," she said softly, "it's okay. Don't be mad."

Then my mother turned to the young woman and said, with the kindest voice I have ever heard, "It's all right, dear. It's not your fault. Just go ahead and get them out. I'll be fine."

+++ +++ +++

I have spent a good deal of my life as a professional advocate. I have used my compassion for the "underdog"—whether that be a creek or a human being with disabilities—to fuel my activism. But activism has often tipped into anger. Compassion has been exclusively directed at one person, one set of circumstances, and not another.

Before that evening, I don't think I'd ever seen so clearly how my anger—righteous anger—closed off possibilities. I don't think I'd ever realized just how powerless others might feel too.

I don't remember much more of that night, except that after my mother spoke to me, my heart felt like it turned over in my chest and started sinking. It sank beneath my need to protect her, beyond my grief and anger and fear, coming to rest in an ocean of admiration and love. That was the moment that I knew, more clearly than ever, that I wanted to be just like my mom when I grew up.

{ 21 }

Not a Problem, Howard

Last fall, in one of those irregular spasms of self-inflicted self-improvement, I picked up Howard Bloom's tome entitled *The God Problem*. Bloom—polymath and paradigm shifter—rolls out the Big Bang; riffs on the formation of matter, molecules, and planets; and slaloms into and out of the intellectual history of the world with an emphasis on mathematics, philosophy, and physics before he closes with God.

Or, more accurately, not God. Bloom scavenges through the past thirteen billion years to argue that the magnificent complexity of the universe is the result of the continued iteration of a few simple axioms. To his way of thinking, this proves there is no God. This is, at least in part, because he has an amazingly limited definition of God as "the old guy in the bathrobe." (Why do so many smart people cling to concepts that would embarrass a preteen fundamentalist? It beggars understanding—but that is a different article.)

Irritation with Bloom's jejune theology aside, the book made some stunning points. Two in particular stuck with me: the impact of iteration and its relationship to implicit properties. When a behavior is repeated—I place a brick on top of another brick, over and over and over and over again—quantum change can occur. Bricks become skyscrapers. Subatomic particles become stars. One-celled animals become antelopes. When some rule like "brick on brick" is reiterated incessantly, something entirely new may come about, something not in the least obvious when I look at a singular brick.

This is more than just piling things up, of course. When repetition comes into play, it has the capacity (although not the certainty) to birth something absolutely unexpected—as the result of an implicit property that had hitherto been hidden. For example, when you repeatedly increase the temperature of H_2O by one degree, it changes from a solid to a liquid and then later to a gas. Who could have predicted that the liquid I drink could expand into a solid I could hand you or simply disappear into vapor? This is not true with other simple compounds, like carbon dioxide or nitrous oxide. While they've got freezing and boiling points too, these are not within the temperature range of normal human experience.

What's fascinating about implicit properties is that we humans are capable of using them before they register in our conscious, intellectual understanding. This is important. If I am attacked by a polar bear, I will want to know what's handy for whacking purposes. I don't need to understand molecular properties to know that a chunk of ice is preferable to a handful of fog or even a bucket of water (although the bucket itself could be nice). In the same manner, the ancient Babylonians, to assure building stability, used a number sequence to measure the adjoining sides of a building and the distance between them. That sequence was 3:4:5. Essentially, they measured off a right angle, but they never articulated the concept of angles, much less the concept of right angles. That came centuries later.

Elizabeth Barrett Browning asserted that "Earth's crammed with Heaven / And every common bush afire with God."[1] Bloom might say that the stuff of this world is crammed with implicit properties, most of which we simply don't recognize—yet.

+++ +++ +++

I'm writing about iteration and implicit properties because that concept has recently saved me. For several weeks, there was something bubbling just below consciousness. I could answer emails, cook dinner, do research, attend meetings, even listen pretty well in spiritual direction. But my writing was turgid, and I couldn't really pray or meditate with any depth. When I would sneak glances at that writhing darkness, it stopped me dead with fear. It looked like despair, and I didn't have the moxie to stare it down.

I knew what to do. I just didn't have the courage to do it. So instead, I screwed around with cultivating curiosity (but not too much) or trying to frame this as part of a bigger picture (but not with much commitment) or remembering (not very regularly) the saints who dealt with despair, like Teresa of Calcutta, who said that our job is not to be successful but to be faithful.

All this can be helpful, but used too soon—shoved into the gap to staunch the wound before I let myself feel—it's just mental sleight of hand, a do-it-yourself project designed to cover over something that really needs to be torn down before it's rebuilt.

So, the tearing-down part finally started last Wednesday. It could have had any trigger—deaths in Nigeria or the latest typhoon victims—but this time it was the environment.

+++ +++ +++

Here in Canada, we have experienced what feels like the Inquisition combined with a slanging match. The Harper government muzzled environmental scientists, closed ocean and freshwater research centers, gutted environmental legislation, and tossed seven libraries of water research into dumpsters. Environmentalists have been labeled terrorists and investigated by Canada Revenue. Steven Harper bashed Neil Young for supporting First Nations resistance to tar-sands mining expansion onto tribal lands. We even have our own nasty little media person who specializes in vicious, inaccurate innuendo and whose favorite target is environmentalist David Suzuki.

Sitting in the doctor's office on Wednesday afternoon—the day after learning that a lake protection plan on which I've been working for seven years was still years from completion—I picked up an old *Macleans* magazine with Suzuki's picture on the front. In the accompanying article, he says that the environmental movement has failed. What with the relentlessness of the cuts, the escalating impacts of climate change, and the personal attacks, it's no wonder he feels that way. I do too, at least sometimes.

When I'm assaulted by despair and denial, they often combine to make me begin believing that praying for the world is ineffectual, recycling is a waste of time, political action is futile, and my lake advocacy hopeless. Despair tells me that nothing can change. Denial says that nothing will change. Because I can't imagine the solution, I begin to believe that there is none.

That's where I was on Thursday morning when it was time to meditate. I simply couldn't hold off the despair any longer. So it was necessity, not virtue, which forced me to dive in, to let the blood flow freely. And necessity taught me once again that what lies deepest within is not despair at all. It is grief, and when I am willing to feel grief, I will discover that it too is simply a surface layer, covering a bottomless ocean of love.

Prayer and meditation are exercises in iteration—the "re" in religion signifies repetition, after all—and deeply spiritual people have always asserted that this repetition changes reality. Chanting short prayers, observing recurrent times of silence and surrender, and the daily exercise of generosity and restraint and fidelity: These shape us, and they shape life around us. Sometimes, these practices bring miniscule change. Sometimes, they birth inconceivable healing. And sometimes, we simply gain the grace to love that which is dark and seemingly beyond repair. Whatever the result, the work serves to bind us to this clement world. Spiritual practices don't guarantee that we get the future we want. They simply open, in us and in the world around us, possibility and relationship.

+++ +++ +++

Last Thursday, when I let down the wall that I had built against my despair and grief, I found myself swimming in an ocean of love. That would have been enough, frankly. But the writing of Howard Bloom, self-professed atheist, gave me even more. I saw the iteration. All across the world, I could see hundreds of thousands—probably hundreds of millions—of people praying, meditating, working to love and cherish every being, every rock, every plant, and every drop of water. I could see the energy of our care connecting, growing, flashing in arcs, blazing around the planet like lightning. I saw our small actions adding up to more than the sum of the parts, creating a web of light, a net of energy, an ocean of possibility.

I felt hope. I felt joy. I felt like I could go on, even if I can't imagine how healing might occur.

And I realized, right then, that the implicit property of prayer revealed by iteration is the same as the implicit property at the heart of the universe: It's Love. If you get the picture right, there ain't no God problem, Howard—there's a God solution.

+++ +++ +++

[1]Elizabeth Barrett Browning, *Aurora Leigh*, Book VII, I, lines 821b–822.

{ 22 }

Hearts at Rest

We have sold Heart's Rest, the retreat center which we built and cared for. While it is a momentous change, it is a change that has been under discussion for several years. To me, it's felt like an interminably long haul from the start of the discussion until now, but the actual time from going live with the house listing to sale was just four months: a lightning strike, according to our real estate agent.

We haven't had the same speed on the other end, finding a new home in this little village. The deal on the wonderful old home we thought we were buying fell apart ten days ago in a welter of asbestos removal and crumbling foundations which we simply couldn't afford. It was so easy to see ourselves in that home that I have found it difficult to wrap my mind around this change—or, I should say, I haven't been able to let my heart feel the change. We've just closed on another property, but the house does not feel as immediately "right" (although the land sure feels good), and we will have a five-week hiatus before moving into our new home. So today, just days from the time we need to be out of here, I'm feeling homeless, without moorings, a little crazy.

+++ +++ +++

This shouldn't be as big a deal as it feels. We can store stuff. Our friends have offered to take us in. We have resources. There are one or two places we could rent in town. We're staying in the same community, after all. But I am finding it almost impossible to keep my soul in any kind of calmness. The best I could do early last week was walk the labyrinth and chant, "Thy kingdom come, thy will be done." That slowed me down for a bit but also reduced me to tears—not necessarily an aid to completion of practical tasks like sorting books or cleaning out drawers or preparing for the retreat I'll be leading at the ashram across the lake in a few weeks.

+++ +++ +++

In my saner moments, I've been contemplating the great difficulty of holding an internal steadiness in the midst of external upheaval. There's a very good reason why monastic orders take vows of physical stability: It is simply easier to go deep into the scary inner places, and stay deep, if the world around you is predictable. (Actually, part of what helps you go deep spiritually is that very outer predictability—it will surely drive you into acedia and thence into more complete surrender, provided you don't go crazy first.) But this experience, this untethering of the outer world, is also a matter of stability and a matter of spiritual practice. Trying to hold on to internal steadiness while the familiar world unravels feels like blackbelt work.

Early last spring, while on retreat, I had a strong sense of needing to root down, get quiet and solid and strong, because a big wind was coming. When four young people of our community drowned in early May, I figured that was the hurricane. I thought, *This is what I have been practicing for*. And it was true—I needed every root clinging in every bit of soil to stay anchored through those days and weeks, to set aside my own grief and stand steady in a world undone.

But that wasn't the end of the storms. All over the world right now, things are flying apart, and it appears that none of us are escaping the personal repercussions. It puts my suffering in perspective—i.e., it is minute—when I read of the masses of people homeless and dying in Syria, Palestine, Ukraine; those dying from Ebola; the contamination and destruction from tar-sand spills in the US and tailing ponds in Canada. Friends are having heart attacks and strokes. Last week, two friends had grandchildren die just before they were born. It feels like the entire world is strained, stressed, and coming apart at the seams. Creation is groaning.

So, how do we stay steady and clear in the midst of such chaos? It is not, I think, a matter of holing up and praying, of distancing ourselves from reality. I will admit that the thought *I could pray better and be better support if my outer life were calmer* often crosses my mind these days. Surely that is true, but it's not really an option. My life isn't calm. Plus, to ask myself not to feel in the midst of this difficult time would be asking for an exemption from the current human condition generally and my own human condition specifically.

I don't have an answer to the question I've just posed: How do we stay steady and clear in the midst of such chaos? I simply have my own experience, my own faltering attempts to hold on.

+++ +++ +++

While packing, I've also been preparing for a retreat based on the sayings of the desert mothers and fathers. In the course of that preparation, I stumbled across one central phrase and an attitude, both of which seem worth hanging on to. The phrase: A desert is any set of constrictions to which we willingly assent. The attitude: Rest (*quies*) is not comfort, absence of motion, or bodily rest. *Quies* is a lack of internal resistance, no matter what the external world brings on.

In light of this, for the past while, I've taken as mantra the phrase, "I say yes." For my patron saint, I've chosen Etty Hillesum, the Jewish Dutchwoman who affirmed, even as she went to her death in a concentration camp, that God is always present and life is wonderfully good. "Tell them we left the camp singing," was her last communication.

When I remember to say that mantra or to think of Etty, the door of my heart swings open. Now, as I pack boxes, say goodbye to the dream of Heart's Rest, feel my heart break as I read the news, work with George to figure out whether we need to replace the roof on the new house before the snow falls, and get ready for a retreat in the midst of all of this, I say yes: yes to this set of constrictions, this desert; yes to the changes and heartbreak; yes to the joy, the silliness, the mess. Yes, yes, yes, I will live this life. Yes, I long to hold the aching world. Yes, I am grateful—beyond all belief—to be alive. Yes, I am afraid of the coming change. Yes, it hurts. Yes, I willingly assent to all this.

+++ +++ +++

My friend Michele reminded me today that we have not sold Heart's Rest, because heart's rest cannot be sold.

When we keep saying yes, it simply lives more deeply inside us. To that too, I say yes.

{ 23 }

Rebellion Dogs

There's a line in an AA book that I love, an invitation to word-play that speaks of the essential difficulty of staying on a spiritual path: "Rebellion dogs our every step."[1]

I recently spent time as a rebellion dog.

Don't ask me why—I could give you reasons galore—but the fact of the matter is that one day recently I stopped meditating, stopped praying, and stopped eating my vegetables. These are the outward signs, if you like, of inward resistance.

A while later, I stopped stopping. I got back at it, started doing all the things that actually make me happy and cause me to feel like part of the human race, the humming exchange of the biosphere.

Yesterday, I saw a woman who was dithering about going to a meditation workshop. She told me, "I am undisciplined and can't maintain a practice."

My answer to that was, "So what? That's what it is to be a human." We stop, we start. We rebel, we return. That is the nature and the joy of life. The problem is not with stopping. The problem is with not starting again.

+++ +++ +++

Our dog Dolly is a marshmallow. Streaky blond with dark eye markings and a pink striped nose, she's good looking and cheerful. Everyone is her best friend. One member of the contemplative group refers to her as the ultimate canine spiritual director. A friend said that the only thing to fear from Dolly is that she will lick you to death.

This is why it always surprises me when she gets in a snit and refuses to obey. She will sit sphinxlike in the yard, intent on a suspected mouse habitation, cutting her eyes at me when I call her in. She will crouch behind a beach log with a prized stick in her mouth and stare. She will lie on the floor with her head turned away, studiously ignoring repeated commands to sit up and get her teeth brushed. I guess it's just hard sometimes to be so good. She must get sick of it.

I try not to get too worried about this behavior. I figure that every dog needs to rebel once in a while. Sooner or later, she always realizes that she wants to be with me, the source of all good things (except mice). Sooner or later, she'll remember that she loves me.

And me? I'm always so glad to see her, to feel her nose my leg to check that I am close, that I can't stay irritated.

+++ +++ +++

Some of my deepest work is to resist judging myself over those moments of rebellion dog. Of course, I want to halt the painful insurrection when it's going on because, frankly, it leaves me miserable and depleted. But calling myself names or wallowing in how bad I am? That's the best way I know to prevent my return to practice. My self-flagellation is just one more way to close out the love of God.

There's a reason why Jesus talked about forgiving sins when he was healing. It's not because everyone he touched was inherently bad and irredeemably screwed up. More likely, it's because he recognized how self-hatred keeps the Holy locked out.

So, when the revolution comes and the howling starts, I try not to get too excited. Rebellion dogs—gotta love 'em, gotta forgive 'em, gotta trust that they will come on home, in their own time, to the deep, deep Love that waits.

+++ +++ +++

[1]Alcoholics Anonymous, *Twelve Steps and Twelve Traditions* (Alcoholics Anonymous World Services, 1981) 73.

{ 24 }

Why I Meditate

I don't meditate to improve my mental acuity. I don't meditate to slow down the effects of aging. I don't meditate to lower my blood pressure, reduce my stress, or improve my frame of mind. I don't meditate to be a better Christian or a nicer human being.

Sure, all of these can be byproducts of my meditation practice. But that's all they are, byproducts, and to say that they're why I meditate is to totally miss the point, like saying that I wear glasses because I am fond of the way the frames look on my face. It may be true that I like how I look in my cute little orange cat-eye frames. But I wear glasses because without them, I am unable to function fully in the world.

I meditate because I am, in a sense, blind without it. Without the surrender inherent in my practice, I lose my deepest vision, my insight. I lose the ability to see myself and the world with the compassion, the forgiveness, and the humility of God.

+++ +++ +++

Here are some other thoughts about my practice: I do not meditate to have insights or mystical experiences. My practice is not measured by how I feel or what I experience when I sit in place for a twenty-minute session. The true test of my practice is my behavior the other twenty-three-plus hours of the day.

A practice is just that: a practice. By definition, a practice gets me ready to do something else. One person practices scales on the piano so she can play a concerto beautifully. Another practices French so that he can converse easily. I practice Centering Prayer so that when life is coming apart at the seams, I remember how to stand steady. I practice Centering Prayer so that I can learn how to stand aside and let God work in and through me.

+++ +++ +++

One more metaphor. Meditation practice can turn me into a sponge. The true nature of a sponge is that it gathers up water and it releases water. It does not hold onto, own, or create water. A living sponge depends on the constant movement of water through its body to stay alive. It is simply filled and then releases that with which it's been filled.Or take your common kitchen sponge, which is wetted, squeezed, and then used to wipe down a counter. It also gathers up and disperses water. That's its purpose.

Or consider those tiny pink sponges on white sticks. More than once I have sat beside the bed of a dying loved one and dabbed their mouth with a damp sponge, trying to relieve parched and desiccated lips. These sponges, too, are intended to gather and disperse water.

In meditation, I am filled with the grace of God, the flowing water of life. (If I am lucky, I will actually experience this in some way. But whether I consciously experience that grace or not, it is always true that I am filled with it.) Hence, the only goal I can truly name for my meditation practice is this: to let myself be filled, over and over, so that I can act as a streaming, saturated sponge, leaking Love in a dry and dusty world.

{ 25 }

Thank You, Limbic System

I've been a meditator for about half of my life. You may want to take that with a grain of salt, as this does not mean that I have been consistent, or good at it, or that I am particularly enlightened or holy. It's just something I have tried to do since my early thirties because it changed me.

In the beginning, it made me feel great. I had those exciting times and beautiful experiences that most early meditators have. My longing for more of the same kept me faithful. But after a few years, meditation settled out into not much of anything, not much in the way of smells, bells, or whistles. I tried changing the kind of meditation I practiced, but that didn't help. I stopped for a while, but that was even worse. When I started back at it, I discovered that instead of getting "better," my practice felt even drier. It seemed like I couldn't concentrate at all. I finally settled into a bleak faithfulness, where my job was simply to catch myself when I wandered off and to forgive myself as I came back to the task. It felt like all I did was practice constant self-compassion.

+++ +++ +++

Somewhere along the line, I realized that while nothing very exciting happened while I was meditating, things were changing elsewhere. It felt easier to be kind at home. I didn't lose my temper so quickly. I could step back from my own feelings instead of getting wound up. When I wondered about why this was so—when I took this personal observation to what I was learning about the brain and meditation—I learned that compassion involves the limbic system, which does not distinguish between self and other. Every time I was not-judging myself, I was strengthening a neural network of generalized not-judging. The emotional/spiritual change in my behavior toward myself and others coincided with a change in my neural pathways. Spirituality is not separate from the body, after all: We are incarnate beings. We live out our practice in this concrete reality.

Over the years, this not-judging has yielded immeasurable peace of mind. By not-judging, I don't mean that I've lost the ability or the willingness to discriminate between right and wrong. It simply means that I can usually do so without attaching hate or contempt to the observation. I can separate the person from the behavior—usually.

+++ +++ +++

A few years ago, a brave young woman, a friend of George's, started holding a vigil across from a permanent picket of Yellow Vest-ers. At that time, the Yellow Vest group took a distinctly anti-immigration, anti-environmental, militant stance.

This young woman talked about standing across the street from the picketers, feeling not only fear but also loathing. Her fear has an obvious source: She is a small woman, and these were big, rowdy men spoiling for a fight. Loathing is a more complex emotion, involving not only intense dislike but disgust, a judgment that someone else's very being is defective and repellent.

It was the loathing that bothered her, she said. She was ashamed of it.

+++ +++ +++

I get it. These days, this is where the rubber meets the road for me. I can catch myself most of the time at home and in family relationships. But the current hateful politics, the sensationalist and fabricated communications of our time, the disdainful attitudes of some Christians and some atheists, vaxxers and anti-vaxxers—I feel loathing every time I run up against people who deny that there is any decency in those whom they oppose. The joke, of course, is that my loathing mirrors theirs. It's an endless carnival fun house, designed to reflect anger, hatred, and suffering ad infinitum.

Someone has to break the mirror. If I am serious about the health of my soul, it has to be me.

+++ +++ +++

So, today I am praying for the particular group by whom I am most upset, that they may experience the love of the Holy. Tomorrow, I hope to have the will to do it again, or maybe to pray for certain political figures. I will not pray that they change—although I sincerely long for that. But I've had people tell me that they were praying for me, when what they meant was that they thought I was a terrible person in need of correction. Prayer, in their mind, was a way to force me to face my error. That's not prayer!

When I pray, I will pray that these people whom I abhor may experience the Infinite Love and that I may see something in them that will call out my compassion. From there, it's God's job to work with them, and it is my job to find the activities that I can pursue, in love, to transform the impact of their abuse.

{ 26 }

View from the Machine

I'm lying on my stomach on a bare metal tray: wedge under my ankles, pillow under my belly, forehead resting on a rolled-up towel. My right arm is extended overhead and locked inside a bulky brace. I've been instructed that I should not move. No part of my body should twitch, wiggle, shift, or budge one single centimeter for the next forty minutes.

I had waited a year for this medical test. But when the day finally rolled around, George was exhausted from a long drive, so I made the four-hour round trip by myself. This was no big deal, except that it meant I didn't take those little relaxing pills that they so gently recommend if you're going to spend any length of time in an MRI machine.

Did I mention that in my left hand was the panic button and that I really, really wanted to use it?

+++ +++ +++

I am not a stranger to panic attacks, although—thanks be to God—I can count the serious ones on a single hand. The most dramatic was remedied by desperate prayer combined with the presence and understanding of a good friend. Because of that, I've had a formula, so to speak, to deal with rising anxiety for the last thirty years. However, once you've found yourself immobilized with fear and unable to walk out the door, life shifts dramatically. It's hard to forget that terrifying paralysis and hard not to fear its return.

So, lying there on that steel slab, when my breathing got hinky, I knew what was happening—or, I should say: I knew what might be happening and felt myself becoming afraid.

It might be that anxiety took hold because I found it impossible to meditate, which is what I had planned on doing while trapped inside the MRI. It might have been because a weird nerve response to the magnets clanking all around caused the crown of my head to feel so hot that it seemed ready to burst into flames. It might have been the loud and unpredictable noises, or the fact that I was pinned face-down inside a machine that I was unable to exit, or the headache that blossomed the minute I stretched out on that table. Whatever the trigger was, I could not get control of my breathing. I couldn't stop the wild beating of my heart.

So I prayed.

Years of experimentation have taught me that in really rough spots, prayer that begs for the relief of my own pain does not "work." That kind of prayer just keeps me focused on my suffering. I'm not saying that I didn't try it! I did. I also asked Jesus to be next to me—and he was. But I felt called into something more, some practice more proactive than simply hanging on with my fingernails until it was all over.

Some of my more enlightened friends would have used this situation to sink deeply into gratitude for this slight medical discomfort—a real first-world problem—but I couldn't manage that. What I seized on is the most powerful practice I know. Its Buddhist name is tonglen. I've called it kything. Over the years, I've come to think of it as a form of contemplative solidarity.

If you don't know this practice, here's a précis: You imagine the suffering of specific others in some visual way, like thick black smoke. You breathe it in, naming what you're doing: Breathe in suffering. Breathe it all the way down, deep into the center of your being. Then you breathe out, and you name that too: Breathe out peace. While this might sound terrifying, it isn't—because the "I" that is breathing in and out isn't my ego self. The one breathing isn't that little individualist who feels responsible for the whole world and who is terrified that she's going to get sick from this. The "I" that breathes in the suffering and breathes out the peace is the deepest, truest place in myself—in Thomas Merton's words, the *pointe vierge*, the place where the Infinite Holy and the particularity of me are indistinguishable. I don't control this place, but I do have access to it. For me, this is what it means to put on the mind of Christ—or, for that matter, Buddha mind. This is participation in the body of Christ.

+++ +++ +++

As I began the practice, those deafening and unpredictable noises provided the raw material to move me into solidarity with other beings. I found myself accompanying whales in their habitats as they were subjected to the loud underwater blasts of military testing and oil exploration. I was breathing in the unpredictability of the noise, the confusion, the inability to escape, and the fear that it would never cease. I was breathing in their grief. And then I was breathing out peace, which felt like a deep acknowledgment that none of us was alone in our pain. As I moved between in-breath and out-breath, what welled up in me was sorrow inseparable from love.

Later on, I found myself with the children confined in cages at the US border: breathing in loss and confusion and helplessness. Breathing in heartbreak. Breathing in fear. And for each in-breath of pain, breathing out peace. Again, a place of deep and paradoxical loss and love.

It is reasonable to ask here if I was just taking a spiritual bypass. I've considered this pretty seriously, and my answer is no. I wasn't avoiding my own pain, anxiety, or fear. I simply felt myself to be part of the family of life, shoulder to shoulder (or flipper to flipper, I guess) with those other beings, my suffering a dim mirror of their own. My own situation became less difficult because I saw that what I was going through in my little drama was the reality for all life. When I carried my own anxiety, I lightened everyone's burden. When I helped carry another's pain, my own lifted. We were in it together.

This is the weird thing about any kind of contemplative solidarity. All this dwelling in these anguished situations with other suffering beings would reasonably seem to be a recipe for despair. But it doesn't feel like that at all. When I do this practice, it feels like joy.

+++ +++ +++

A cedar stump taught me about this practice.

A number of years ago, I attended a retreat in Washington state. The center where we stayed had been struggling to stay solvent. In a desperate attempt at financial security, the board of directors had contracted for a large part of their old-growth forest to be logged—clear-cut, actually: a shocking surprise when I turned off the highway onto the long road to the lodge. The land felt desolated. It seemed right to avert my eyes. When we had time in the retreat schedule to walk, everyone headed uphill toward the remaining woods rather than toward the abused slopes below.

But one day, I decided to find the fabled waterfall noted on the dining hall map. While getting there involved a hike across the clear-cut area, the manager assured me that it would be worth it. He swore that I would find it easily by listening for the roar. And no, he hadn't been out there since the logging was complete, but he had been assured that they would preserve that area.

So, off I slogged across the grim ground, over and around stumps and limbs, gullies and washouts, trying to ignore the destruction all around me. I assumed that I'd find some stand of virgin forest around the side of the hill, but there was none. I finally stumbled into a tiny glen tucked into a fold of the slope, right in the middle of the clear-cut. The waterfall was barely a trickle. The formerly lush greenery was dying for lack of moisture. Where I expected to taste cool spray, I could only taste dust and death.

I climbed back out and looked closely at the churned-up land. I could see that the feeder creek for the waterfall was nearly extinct. The rain—formerly husbanded by trees and undergrowth into a stream—now tore down the hill as runoff, slumps, and mudslides. There wouldn't be a stable watercourse here for years and years. Life wouldn't flourish in the tiny valley for a long time. The machinery of financial need had killed it.

I wandered through the clear-cut, touching the huge stumps, asking for forgiveness. I felt shame for humanity, so heedless of the consequences we set in motion. Almost automatically, I began to breathe in the sound of saws, the violence and the falling, the mudslides, the death of the creek, and the death of the forest. I breathed in powerlessness and deep sorrow. I wept.

I was sitting down on the remnants of a cedar tree, drained, when I felt some kind of invitation. The cedar stump was addressing me, encouraging me to move beyond self-hatred. It was offering me solace and welcoming me into the family of all living beings. We were kin. While we were sharing the sorrow, the spirit of that tree was also reminding me of the joy that was our mutual ground and source. That bare stump *took me* to that mutual ground and source, where I was awash in the energy of love.

I burst into tears again, but this time it was for joy.

+++ +++ +++

I am always curious about the conceptual correlates of prayer practices. I really do like to see that there is consistency between what I think I am doing spiritually and what I know about how humans think. I don't assume that neural activation is causal for every bit of my prayer experiences, but there is clearly a correlation between what my neurons are doing and what I experience. From experience, I know that shifting what I am able to shift—changing my conceptual framing of a given situation—can make an opening for an experience of the Ineffable.

So, as I have revisited these two experiences, I've tried to see what is involved in the move out of self-centered fear or sorrow into a sense of oneness. Inside the MRI machine, my initial motivation was my own fear. In the clear-cut, I began with grief. But the end place for both situations was the same: a space of joyful unity.

If I use Cynthia Bourgeault's framework, the transition would be from the egoic operating system to a unitive operating system. I move from experiencing the world as fragmented and dangerous into the nondual mind, the Christ mind. I begin to see from the heart.

If I use the theories of conceptual framing, contemplative solidarity turns the traditional understanding of prayer on its head. Just think about the garden variety understanding of prayer: it's initiated by a person who is disturbed by a situation (which may involve only themselves). The person takes action by petitioning a god for cessation of the situation. The present is odious, the change uncertain. It's all about me, or maybe it's about someone I love. It's all about not-now. It's all about getting out of this mess. It can be a tiny little world, this world of traditional prayer.[1]

By contrast, contemplative solidarity starts with a "long, loving look at the real"[2]—what I am really experiencing, what you are really experiencing. It's about the big picture, and it's thoroughly rooted in the present moment. Instead of petitioning an outside source for a quick change, we sink into simply *being with*. We recollect, in heart and mind, that everything and everyone has its origin in the same Ground. Instead of looking outside for some other power to change a noxious situation, we use the suffering as a doorway into joyous recognition of our inseparability. When we breathe in pain, we breathe in what all of life experiences: God along with us. When we breathe out peace, we breathe out what resides deeply in us, i.e., the Holy Ineffable. The trajectory of the conceptual frame is not toward some future cessation of pain. It is instead an embrace of the present at all its levels. It is a dwelling together in our suffering. That dwelling together in suffering opens the door to a dwelling together in the Divine Joy.

It's that Divine Joy that binds our beating hearts together, whether those hearts are human hearts or mammalian hearts or the heartwood of a clear-cut cedar.

+++ +++ +++

[1]Please don't mistake what I am saying. Prayer is not intended to be a tiny world. It's when we think we can use prayer as a kind of magical talisman, a formula to order life the way we prefer it, that prayer shrinks us and the world around us. I am well aware that intercessory prayer can rip our hearts open and shake the world—but that's not garden variety prayer, that's a leap into a different reality. And that kind of prayer still begins with a long, loving look at the real.

[2]This quote comes from William McNamara, OCD, and is the title of the second chapter in his book *The Human Adventure: Contemplation for Everyman* (Doubleday, 1974).

PART IV: AND THEY DRAW FROM THE HEAVENS LIGHT

{ 27 }

Holding the Post

I recently went up Red Mountain Road to drop off some jam for friends. Their driveway being an impassable pile of snow, I parked below and followed a trail up the side of the mountain through a tract of mature forest.

I *felt* those woods before I really saw them. Something made me stop, take in the girth of the trees, tip back my head, and stare up through the canopy of sacred space: aspen and cedar and hemlock trunks too thick to be spanned with two sets of arms, overstory forming a separate ecosystem, lungwort lichen everywhere, the air so sweet you could taste it. That forest was steadfast, "holding its post," as a teacher of mine says. I could feel the deep roots drinking from the underground creek, connected by fungi, exchanging secret messages. I could see the flexible, sturdy trunks upholding the breathing crowns. I could sense the web of animal communities sheltering in and around those trees.

+++ +++ +++

I was thinking about that Red Mountain forest this week when I walked a trail near our house. I couldn't help comparing the woodlands on my path to that sylvan site. Many of the trees here are spindly, crowded, or bent over with a wasting disease. The larger ones often have dead crowns or cankers bursting their bark. Pines drip sap tears and rusted needles. Recent windstorms have toppled big hemlocks with root rot. Last year's deep snow snapped off the tops of healthy firs. As I looked, I felt my heart turning away from these diseased, scrawny specimens. I found myself bemoaning the sickly forest.

Then something inside me asked, *Who are you to judge?*

It came to me, as soon as that voice spoke, that these trees, too, were holding their post. They provide what shelter they can for birds and small animals. They spend their days breathing in and out so that others can breathe. They attempt to stand both flexible and steadfast. Within the limitations of the place in which they find themselves—with diseases in the soil, with fire and logging and drought, with invasive species borne on the boots of walkers like me—they live out their purpose as best they can.

It's easy to think that healthy and prominent trees—be they human or arboreal—will save us. Such giants are critical, of course. But individuals alone will not save us. In evolution, change comes through collective magnitudes, not outliers. There is a post for everyone. Everyone is needed.

Some of us might be rooted in thin soil or lack underground water sources. We might be slammed by economic and political issues over which we are powerless. We might struggle with the same diseases that infect the community around us.

I just want to say: Our effort still counts. It is critical to hold the post we have been given, regardless of how slender that post might feel. Even if we're saplings barely hanging on, the work that we do to stand steadfast, to support the community to which we belong, "to breathe in and breathe out. It counts."

+++ +++ +++

{ 28 }

Hidden

The hiddenness of God is one of the two major philosophical challenges to the existence of God. If you're arguing that God is not real—that's "God" in the traditional sense of all-knowing, all-powerful, and all-good—you cite either the existence of evil and suffering or the hiddenness of God to support your disbelief. You say, if God's so good, why can't humans experience God more easily? Why isn't God there when we feel like we desperately need God? Why isn't the evidence plain? All this hiddenness smacks of communal delusion, implying that there's really nothing there.

On this rock, many a faith has foundered, because the answer can't be found in logic. The only answer that makes sense is the mystic's answer, the answer of Job, and that's not really an answer. It's a stance. It's the recognition that my little pea brain can't take in the fullness and broadness of the Holy, any more than a one-celled being can understand me. Job realized that it is the height of human hubris to assume that we should be able to understand. (Of course, then comes this question: What kind of God would make humans so damned dim? But that's some other discussion.)

There is yet another answer to the question of the hiddenness of the Divine. It's found in the experience of the mystics. It's also on display in the new cosmology/theology of our evolving universe. This is the observation that the Holy isn't hidden at all, or—more clearly—God is hidden in plain sight: integral, inseparable from all of life. Pierre Teilhard de Chardin called this the Divine Milieu, where everything participates in the One. Every single situation is of

God. God is being-ness, not a being; experience, not a concept; feeling, not an idea; reality, not a proof.

This leads me to a related kind of hiddenness: not God's hiddenness, but my own.

+++ +++ +++

My reading this past year has been challenging. I struggled
through a lot of Teilhard de Chardin's work—as well as books, articles, podcasts, and blog posts about him—because the contemplative
group wanted a Teilhard retreat. I read *A God that Could Be Real* by
Nancy Ellen Abrams because—when I panned a positive assessment
of the book—I was challenged to write my own review. (I've revised
that assessment, by the way: It's a good book, just ignorant about
the depth of thought in Christianity.) I read *The Innovators* (Walter
Isaacson), a history of the people who developed computers and the
Internet, because George wanted to talk about it together. I don't
know that I would have chosen to read any of these books if I hadn't
had a push.

The end result has been surprising: a new orientation toward the
universe and life. I feel stretched out toward the future, an arrow of
evolution in the endless stream of creativity—but not as a singular
point, a supernova of wisdom and light. This is more like being one
of the crowd.

+++ +++ ++++

I have imbibed the cultural value of individualism pretty deeply.
I remember once thinking that the worst thing that could happen to
me would be to teach at a community college rather than, say, Har-
vard. I was appalled by my experience of student preaching to a
congregation of thirty or forty and swore I'd never take a small
church.

On the scale I set for myself, I've failed quite profoundly: I teach nowhere regularly, and the local church that I serve unofficially has maybe eight members. I have not set the world on fire, made my mark, or become famous and important.

I would be lying if I said that it doesn't bother me sometimes.

+++ +++ +++

One hundred years ago, Teilhard de Chardin started talking about the "reality and organicity of collective magnitudes."[1] In more recent years, biologists and physicists have begun to speak of what they call "emergent properties."[2] Both Teilhard de Chardin and contemporary scientists have observed that when some *thing* (a subatomic particle, atom, molecule, cell, animal, etc.) reaches a critical mass, something new and entirely different results. It is not possible to know beforehand the number of things required to bring about this change. The nature of the new "something" is likewise unpredictable, and the laws that govern this new entity are unforeseeable. The product that results from a collective magnitude will behave in ways and have capacities that cannot be anticipated. "More," as the physicist Phil Anderson says, "is different."[3]

This principle of collective magnitudes—emergent properties—underlies the entire universe. Ever since the Big Bang banged, the movement toward entropy has been opposed by a movement toward increasing complexity and consciousness. Here are a few examples: the emergence of organic life from inorganic elements, the capacity of ant colonies to adjust foraging levels and locations, the organization of muscles into a heart that pumps blood, and the appearance of consciousness. The constituent parts remain the same, remain their full selves—chemicals, ants, muscles, neurons—but when those constituent parts are working together, something radically new can emerge. No single atom of my body is biologically alive, but each participates in life. I am alive.

In evolution, it is collective magnitudes—not outliers—that change reality and set new laws into motion. Outliers are important, but lasting change comes when a sufficient number of individual entities are fully themselves and fully in relationship with each other.

+++ +++ +++

The Hasidic tradition speaks of the *lahmed vav tzadikim*—the thirty-six righteous ones of every generation. Unknown to themselves and to each other, their life of prayer and righteousness makes things right with God. Anonymous, scattered, hidden: Across the continents, they bear the sorrows of humanity. They hold the earth together.

I'm betting that we need more than thirty-six people right now. Looking at the bloody mess of the world, it's obvious that we desperately lack a sense of fertile possibility. Given global distress and dystopic expectations, many minds are thinking the same thing: *We're hooped.* I'm praying there's no collective magnitude living out of this conceptual framework, this expectation that the human being is devolving into a creature without the capacity to respond to life with generosity, possibility, vision, ethical consideration, or beauty.

It is no longer sufficient to trust in some hidden *lamed vavnicks* or to pray for visionaries to lead us. It's time to become visionaries ourselves. When we hold inside ourselves a sense of deep connection to the bigger picture—the possibilities of evolution, the future we can't anticipate but which promises something unimaginably new—and, most importantly, when we trust in the ultimate goodness of life and hold that deep connection in spite of our own fear, uncertainty, despair, and suffering, we become part of evolutionary emergence. We don't know what our work will bring into being. We don't know how many of us it will take. But we can certainly believe that our work is part of some new collective magnitude, an alternative to the devolution that threatens to tear our world apart.

+++ +++ +++

Finally, and importantly, I must remember this: Evolution responds to deeds, not thoughts. I can ponder all these thoughts, but my thinking changes nothing unless it is translated into actions. Choose your own authority, here:

- Thomas Merton: "Christianity does not teach man to attain an inner ideal of divine tranquility... It teaches him to give himself to his brother and to his world in a service of love."[4]
- The Dalai Lama: "It's unrealistic to think that the future of humanity can be achieved through prayer or good wishes alone; what we need is to take action."[5]
- Mahatma Gandhi: "What is faith worth if it is not translated into action?"[6]

No matter how you cut it, we have work to do.

I am well and truly convinced that I must point all of me toward the next great emergence. To that end, I'm writing this. I'm meditating, voting, volunteering, and listening. I'm laughing, loving, and growing things. This is my work. I don't know what your work is, but I do know that we are doing it together, part of a mass of unseen evolutionary revolutionaries trusting blindly in something we can't yet imagine but for which we long.

Hidden here in the backwater of New Denver, British Columbia, population less than 600 souls in a world of 7,726,752,303, I'm the leading edge of evolution—as are you. Wahoo!

+++ +++ +++

[1]Pierre Teilhard de Chardin, *The Heart of the Matter: The Important Spiritual Autobiography of One of the World's Greatest Thinkers* (Harcourt, 1978), 31.

[2]See Nancy Ellen Abrams, *A God That Could Be Real: Spirituality, Science, and the Future of Our Planet* (Beacon Press, 2015), Chapter Two.

[3]Philip W. Anderson, "More is Different," *Science,* 177 (4047), 1972, Pages 93-396. Accessed at https://cse-robotics.engr.tamu.edu/dshell/cs689/papers/anderson72more_is_different.pdf.

[4]Thomas Merton, *Love and Living* (Sheldon Press 1970), 150.

[5] Dalai Lama (@DalaiLama), "It's unrealistic to think that the future of humanity can be achieved only on the basis of prayer, what we need is to take action," https://x.com/DalaiLama/status/322643496961986560, Twitter, April 12, 2013.

[6]D. G. Tendulkar, *Mahatma: Life of Mohandas Karamchand Gandhi,* 2nd ed. (Publications Division, Ministry of Information and Broadcasting, Government of India, 1960), 5:180.

{ 29 }

Doulas to the World

For all creation is groaning in birth pangs together.
Romans 8:22

"It's like I'm a Carmelite nun," she said, "except that I get to have sex every once in a while."

I laughed, because I knew exactly what she meant.

My life is full of women of a certain age. Crones, I have called us, counting myself proudly among that tribe. Graying and wrinkling, we may have cataracts and hearing aids, but we see more and hear more than most people, often more than we want to. Our daily lives are brimming. We've got partners, many of us. We've also got friends with cancer, kids with addictions, elderly parents needing end-of-life care. We are anguished by the consumer economy and the ravaged earth. Some of us are raising our children's children. We discern starvation of body, mind, and spirit everywhere. We see it. We hear it. We get asked to pray about it.

And because we love, we pray.

+++ +++ +++

When we get together to talk, it normally starts with a question that's not really a question, but a cry: How do I deal with all this suffering? Then comes the list of witnessed miseries, the pieces we are trying to hold, the sheer aching injustice of life.

We confess sleeplessness.

We concede powerlessness.

We admit that we can't seem to hang onto a clear picture.

We affirm that there is something fuller, deeper, and more luminous behind all this sorrow.

We always end by talking about our prayer life.

Sometimes, that prayer life feels like a desperate finger plugged into a crumbling dike of chaos. Other times, it's a great shimmering web of grace. Either way, we know that prayer holds things—us—together. Prayer is the response that Love makes in us. Prayer empowers our mundane service. Prayer is our daily *cri de cœur*, married to, and equipping us for, the tedious and tender care of life within our orbit.

Crones, I've called us. But just recently, a new name came to me for praying, graying women: We are doulas.

+++ +++ +++

If you're familiar with the world of birthing, you'll know that a doula (the ancient Greek word for female slave or wet nurse) is the new help needed by every expectant mother. The role formerly relegated to mother, maiden aunt, or really good friend—that of a female companion who provides physical care and emotional support during and after birthing—is now a job description. Although there is a certification process, medical training isn't required, but rather the capacity to serve, to stand calm in the midst of tumult. Think cool-cloth-on-sweaty-forehead, cheesy-macaroni-when-you've-forgotten-to-eat kind of attention.

Unlike birthing doulas, praying doulas aren't certified. We are housewives, nuns, environmental activists, dancers. We are chaplains, artists, teachers, doctors. We are musicians, weavers, engineers, therapists. Whatever our work, our central qualification for doulahood is not the result of professional training. We have learned our trade through the exercise of constancy and forgiveness, through experiences of grief and grace. Surrender is our most important tutor. Silence is our home. Our most important attribute is the willingness to love and carry on when things seem hopeless.

Because this work of ours is not hopeless.

This is a birth to which we are attending.

The groaning we hear is creation in labor pains, not death throes.

+++ +++ +++

Embedded in all of creation is a throbbing thrust toward becoming. Some people call it evolution. I call it the Love that Pulses at the Center of the Universe, aka God. Whatever you call it, it's important to recognize that death is not the whole story. Neither is it the last story.

Remembering that we are handmaids to birth is a difficult task. It requires constant pushing against the collective culture of death, pushing against the fear that we humans are the walking dead. Yes, we are drowning in our own waste. Yes, we are poisoning our earth. Yes, every crack and weak link seems to bloom with disorder and decay. However, if collapse and degradation become the only collective story for these difficult days, we're screwed. Because what we cannot imagine cannot come into being. If we don't have a conceptual frame—a new story—that contains birth, we won't be able to recognize the nascent life that is rising from these ashes.

Our doula job is to remember that the spark of life is indeed present in this disorder and pain and to work and pray to bring this nativity into being.

The writhing of our times is real. But ultimately, no matter how many deaths and extinctions we are called to witness, we are here to serve the birthing.

{ 30 }

Whole Hearted

I roll over to turn off the light and address a silent prayer to my deepest part, to the Holy, to my unconscious, to whatever or whomever prescribes the nightly play that goes on when I slump into sleep: *May I please have some joy in my dreams tonight?*

I've been tired, bone tired. The recent big crisis is resolved, at least for a while. But crises never really end, do they? When the immediate situation gets better—someone gets out of the psych ward, someone gets into treatment, the rains put the fires out, someone dies after the long illness—then the dam that held everything back starts to leak. The feelings start: the tears, the sadness, the heavy darkness kept at bay by the need to just keep going.

It's not simply that crises don't really end. It's also that when life settles, it never settles back to how it was. I'm changed. There's a bit more of a broken heart. If I do my work, there's a bit more tenderness too.

And as I have been occupied with the suffering in my immediate bubble, the wars in Ukraine and the Middle East go on, the executions in Iran go on, the discovery of unmarked graves of Indigenous children goes on, the killing of black men in the US goes on, the destruction of the environment goes on. All those bass notes of despair are sounding in the background.

Hence my plea for joy.

+++ +++ +++

I am in a room, a performance space, sitting in the back, watching a musical contest. Every entrant—me included—is supposed to sing the same glorious song. The original is utterly light, pitch perfect, sublimely beautiful. Think Jacob Collier at his best. Everyone loves to sing this song.

Hanging from the stage is a swing dress: bright red, short, covered in tiny lights. The lights are linked to the notes of the deceptively simple and haunting chorus. On the right side of the stage there is a line of contestants that goes on forever. Each one will put on that scarlet dress and sing, the lights glowing softly as they hit the notes.

Each and every contestant is killing it.

When I say that the contestants are killing it, I don't mean that they are doing a great job. They are singing their hearts out, it's true. They are also singing off-key, off-tempo, off-everything. I've never heard worse singing in my life, including and especially my own awful attempt. It is so unbelievably bad, it's killing *me*. I fall out of my chair, laughing. Looking up at the One who organized the contest, I say, "I love you so much! Thank you for organizing this—it's so much fun! I just love you!"

I am laughing so hard that I wake myself up.

+++ +++ +++

Dacher Keltner of the Greater Good Science Center in Berkeley, California recently published findings from a study examining common triggers for awe. The research collaborators found that humans experience awe most deeply when in the presence of moral beauty: when we see other humans be courageous, truthful, and generous; when we experience someone motivated by purity of intention and action. Moral beauty inspires us. This is true, regardless of the culture in which we live, the age group or social niche or financial class to which we belong. Other people's goodness breaks us open. It takes us to a place vast and mysterious, full of joy and awe.

+++ +++ +++

Here in Canada, red dresses carry deep significance. Jaime Black, the Métis artist whose REDress project inspired the Red Dress movement, hung empty red dresses for her art installation about murdered and missing Indigenous women. She chose red because of the way the color grabs the attention, evoking vitality as well as violence. She also chose red to reflect the Canadian Indigenous belief that red is the only color spirits can see. To hang up an empty red dress is not only to remember the dead, but to invite the spirits of the lost to reconnect with the living.[1]

+++ +++ +++

It took a while to completely understand my dream. When the meaning arrived, fully formed, I dissolved into laughter again—but also into tears.

I saw that each of us has a melody planted within, a deep invitation to wholeness encoded in flesh and bone. Donning that scarlet swing dress is the way we say, "I'm showing up for my life, body and soul, lost parts included."

And each and every one of us fucks that song up royally. We butcher the music in our very own, entirely unique way. We go up when we should have gone down. We prolong the staccato note, belt out the pianissimo part, miss the sharp, add a flat. We can't hang onto the rhythm, and we forget the chorus. We are wholeheartedly awful.

But by God, we are wholehearted.

How courageous, how endearing it is to stand up in that starlit, scarlet dress and earnestly sing our hearts out! How can hearts not crack open, awed at the effort that we are each putting into this impossible task? I howl with laughter while the tears run down my cheeks, gasping at the sheer beauty of everyone who is trying to heal the world, heal ourselves, find our way.

+++ +++ +++

[1]]See https://www.thecanadianencyclopedia.ca/en/article/red-dress-day. Racialized, sexualized violence against Indigenous women, girls, and gender-diverse persons is a fact of life in Canada. The Assembly of First Nations reports that Indigenous women are four times more likely than non-Indigenous women to be   victims of violence. While Indigenous people comprise only 4.3% of Canada's population, Indigenous women make up 11% of all missing women, and 16% of all female homicide victims. The Federal Inquiry on Murdered and Missing Indigenous Women and Girls finished its work in 2019, but change is very slow. In 2023, an article in The Lancet names the situation as a pediatric health crisis (https://www.the-lancet.com/journals/lanchi/article/PIIS2352-4642(23)00135-9/full-text), while the Assembly of First Nations notes, in 2025, that we have yet to see real, on the ground changes. The violence against Indigenous women is inextricably tied into the displacement and destruction of Indigenous community and culture evidenced by colonization, broken treaties, residential schools, ongoing racial discrimination and extraction economies. For more information, see https://nwac.ca, https://afn.ca/rights-justice/murdered-missing-indigenous-women-girls/, https://www.mmiwg-ffada.ca/home-page/ and https://macleans.ca/lost-and-broken/.

Therese DesCamp started writing at the age of seven, and hasn't stopped yet. She has written essays, articles, reflections and reviews for Willamette Week, the Journal for the Study of the Pseudepigrapha, "The Holy Ghost-writer," Religious Studies News, the Journal of Pastoral Psychology, the Monterey Herald, the United Church Observer, Broadview Magazine, and the Valley Voice newspaper. She was long-listed for the 2023 CBC Nonfiction Prize, and has received awards for her scholarship, research, and teaching from the Graduate Theological Union in Berkeley, California and United Theological College, Montreal. Therese has taught at Pacific School of Religion; University of California, Berkeley; Graduate Theological Union; Vancouver School of Theology; and in the Grade 4-5-6 classroom at Lucerne Elementary School in New Denver, B.C. She is a member of the 2020 cohort of the Living School, a program of the Center for Action and Contemplation; works as an ordained minister and spiritual director; and has spent over three and a half decades in twelve-step recovery. Therese lives in New Denver, B.C., where she served ten years on the Slocan Lake Stewardship Society and co-sponsored the Convergence Writers' Retreats from 2012-2019. She currently serves on the board of The Contemplative Society.

Acknowledgments

Writing acknowledgements is a terrifying task. This book has been in process so long that I am sure I have forgotten someone important, probably many someones. So, I start with a heartfelt thanks to everyone whose name doesn't appear below. You will never know how much hope your kind words provided me in the long and lonely work of writing.

As for the rest of you, what is adequate? Surely not the thanks that you will find on this page. I recognize that this is only a start.

To Bill W., Dr. Bob and Nina J., thank you for saving my life. To Annie and Gina and the Tuesday Meditation group and all the women with whom I have prayed all these years, my undying gratitude. To the seasoned writers who encouraged me and pushed me to keep sending this material out into the world—Tom Wayman, Anne DeGrace, Meg DesCamp, Karen Lacey, Alanna Mitchell, Joy Kogawa, Claire Paradis, Karen Price, and Corinne Tessier—my deepest thanks. To the financial angels who believed my writing could be of use to a greater audience—Steve Case, Ken Bernhardt, Jim Ahasay, and the Turner-Zion United Church of Canada in New Denver—a bow of gratitude. Merci to Eloise Charet-Calles, whose memory keeps me honest. To my lovely and oh-so-wise editors, Shirin McArthur, Karen Lacey, Meg DesCamp, and to Conrad Kanagy, publisher with vision and courage, my thanks for your critical and tender eyes. To my dad, who loved words well-turned; to my mom, whose curiosity and intelligence were boundless; to my siblings, all of whom gracefully scribe the word upon the page; and to George, whose support is rock-steady and who sees beauty everywhere: I love you. I thank you.

Book Summary

Hands Like Roots: Notes on an Entangled, Contemplative Life draws its subject matter from roots deep in science, spirituality, and a love of life. This liminal work integrates seemingly disparate knowledge—hydrology, cognitive linguistics, climate instability, embodiment—with the inner experience of prayer and meditation, creating an accessible, poetic, heart-opening whole. Authentic, impassioned, intelligent and vulnerable, *Hands Like Roots* is a real love story about a human heart and the Heart of the Ineffable.

www.ingramcontent.com/pod-product-compliance
Lightning Source LLC
Chambersburg PA
CBHW061751120626
46550CB00005B/1953